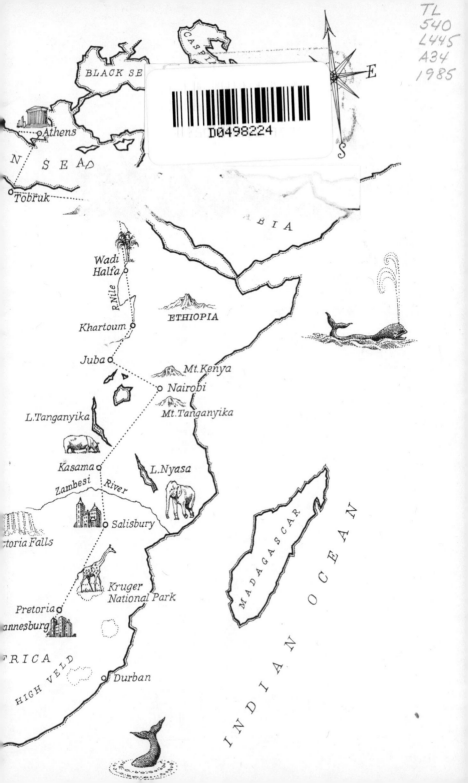

BLACK SE

CAS

N   E

Athens

N   S E A

Tobruk

A B I A

*Wadi
Halfa*

R. Nile

ETHIOPIA

Khartoum

Juba

Mt. Kenya

Nairobi

L. Tanganyika

Mt. Tanganyika

Kasama   River

Zambesi

L. Nyasa

Salisbury

ctoria Falls

*Kruger
National Park*

Pretoria
annesburg

M A D A G A S C A R

O C E A N

FRICA   HIGH VELD

Durban

I N D I A N   O C E A N

Gemini to Joburg

Broadcasting from Within (1924)
Sagittarius Rising (1936)
The Trumpet Is Mine (1938)
Challenge to The Night (1938)
Pathfinders (1943)
Yesterday's Evenings (1946)
Farewell to Wings (1964)
Turn Right for Corfu (1972)
Never Look Back (1974)
A Way to Be (1977)

Gemini to  Joburg

Cecil Lewis

RANDOM HOUSE ⌂ NEW YORK

Copyright © 1984 by Cecil Lewis
All rights reserved under International and Pan-American
Copyright Conventions.
Published in the United States by Random House, Inc., New
York.

Library of Congress Cataloging in Publication Data
Lewis, Cecil, 1898–
Gemini to Joburg.
1. Lewis, Cecil, 1898–   . 2. Air pilots—
Great Britain—Biography. I. Title.
TL540.L445A34 1985   629.13′092′4 [B]   84-15888
ISBN 0-394-54321-1

Manufactured in the United States of America
24689753
First Edition

TO ALL THOSE
WHO MAKE A LONG JOURNEY AND
COME BACK
TO WHERE THEY ARE
AND SEE IT ALL ANEW.

Foreword

We all have two lives, an outer with which we face the world, an inner with which we (sometimes) face ourselves.

This book is about a short period in my life during which I undertook an exciting extrovert adventure: to fly—with my wife—a small airplane from England to South Africa. But the flight was undertaken under the drive of a far deeper motive—to preserve a fragment of a new religious teaching for posterity.

Two more unlikely aims were perhaps never combined before. But slowly and strangely they began to interpenetrate each other. In the long hours flying high above the terrible deserts "peopled only by silence and the spirit of God," in the uncharted endless swamps and jungles of equatorial Africa, the inner aim began to find a place in the outer, and the serenity and fathomless beauty of our aerial world to form a fitting setting for this inner jewel—which, though in a way we did not know what it was, remained the shining matrix of the whole.

Contents

Gemini to Joburg

1

To Paris

PREPARE FOR TAKEOFF! It wasn't exactly an order, but it implied a sequence of quite specific routines that pilots and crews went through before taking the air. In the First World War it was, as I remember it, extraordinarily casual. You just climbed into the cockpit, did up your belt, moved the controls about to see if they were free. Then you shouted loudly to your fitter that the engine switches were OFF—he could be killed if the engines started accidentally. No need to check that the petrol, and oil tanks were full. That would have been looked after by your own chaps—and there were no gauges anyway. When he had "sucked in" the engine by turning the prop backwards, by hand, your fitter would call "Contact!" You switched the engine on and called "Contact!" back to him. He gave the propeller blade an almighty heave and, with luck, the engine started. After a few seconds to warm up, you waved away the chocks and taxied off downwind to the hedge at the bottom of the field (no runway, of course, just good green grass), turned into wind, looked around to make sure there was nobody coming in to land, pulled down your goggles, asked your passenger if he was all right, pushed open the throttle and took off.

By the time the Second World War came along it had all got a bit more complicated, though it still kept a laconic air. Aircrews were so skilled and professional that it was part of the "form" to appear casual about matters on which you could afford no mistakes. Besides, aircraft had become far more complicated and the dangers greater. By the end of the war, books were needed to list all the actions necessary for a safe takeoff. Enthusiasm had been clobbered by responsibility, sport had become a profession and nothing was much fun anymore.

But it sometimes happens that little backwaters get overlooked and left behind. So for a few years after the Second World War a handful of fortunate pilots still flew their private aircraft, pretty well unhampered by the civil flying regulations that were then building up. We too had our simple routines, and since they will soon be swept away, like the airplanes we flew, into the limbo of history,

I take this opportunity of detailing the takeoff routine for
the Miles Gemini, a prototype of a light four-seater execu-
tive aircraft, in the autumn of 1947.

The Miles Gemini was a wooden aircraft of beautiful
design. Her tanks held fuel for six hours' flying, and at a
speed of 120 m.p.h., this gave a range of about 800 miles.
She had a ceiling of 12,000 feet, could just maintain height
on one engine and had lovely big flaps that brought the
landing speed down to 35 m.p.h. Altogether she was a
little beauty. It was a pleasure to walk around her to admire her sleek lines and also, incidentally, to check the tire
pressures in undercarriage and tailwheel, with a pause at
each engine pod to look for telltale oil drips which could
mean a leak of precious oil from our four-cylinder inverted
Cirrus engines. Nothing. So we might as well get cracking.
The cockpit doors in the Gemini lifted sideways from a
central top hinge. Sliding under them into the left-hand
seat, the pilot found all his instruments before him. His
seat was separated from his passenger's by Trim Control.
In front of the passenger's seat were shelves and lockers
for maps, gloves, dusters, etc. Behind the two front seats
were another two, and the whole cockpit—the size of a
Mini—had big perspex windows with a wonderful all-
round view.

Now for the morning check. Electrics ON. Main-engine
switches OFF. Petrol ON. The needles on the gauges slide
up to show FULL. Wind the Clock. Set the altimeter to
zero, but check the height of the airfield at the next stop,

which might be 1,000 feet higher. If it was, set your altimeter to 1,000 feet NOW; people could get badly caught out
on this making an approach in dirty weather.

Now to run up the engines. Brakes hard ON. Main
switches, port engine, ON. Throttle one-third OPEN.
Starter button DEPRESS. The little prop begins to struggle
around. She catches. Throttle back to tickover. Same routine for the starboard motor. The Cirrus was a 90-h.p.
air-cooled engine. No need to warm it up. So, after thirty
seconds, open up to two-thirds full power to check the
magnetos. Cut out each in turn. No drop in revs. Okay.
Now a burst of full power to check revs and oil pressures.
Throttles back to tickover. Fine.

Close all windows and lock them shut. Wave away
chocks (if any). Brakes OFF. Juggle the throttles to steer
downwind to the leeward side of the field. At 90° to wind,
STOP. Brakes ON. VITAL ACTIONS. Set 20° flap. Trim neu-
tral. All controls tested and moving freely. Seatbelts tight.
Airfield clear for takeoff. I turned to Olga (my wife).

"All set? Here we go."

On my releasing the brakes and steadily pushing open
the starboard throttle, the Gemini would turn into wind.
Then, both engines giving full power, she would slowly
gather way, lift her tail, reach flying speed, and I would
ease her off. Once airborne, a flip of a switch to retract the
undercart. When the two lights showed green, the legs
were locked up. Now ease back the flaps till they were
fully up. The Gemini would sink a little when you did this,
taking up her true flying attitude and gaining speed. By

now we would be up to 500 feet, time to check around the instruments, set a compass course from the map and settle down to a steady climb at 70 m.p.h.

Such was our takeoff routine, made special that October morning in 1947 as our destination was Johannesburg, 6,000 miles away.

•

We were 3,000 feet over the Reigate Gap when my wife began to betray those small signs of agitation which usually mean that something is "up."

She looked around her carefully, knelt on the seat to examine all the suitcases piled up behind us, and then resumed her place by my side. She was deep in thought.

"My make-up case—it isn't here. We must have left it . . ."

"Too bad!"

My reaction was immediate. Furious. Setting out like this on a great adventure—on a great Epic Flight!—and, within an hour, after a euphoric send-off from family and friends, here we were, metaphorically slipping on a banana peel, falling flat on our faces over a make-up case!

"Sorry, sweetie, but we must go back."

"Not on your life. You can pick up what you need in Paris."

"But all my jewelry—my things . . ."

I could see the situation growing in her mind. All those miles of air. The tropics, the heat, the dust—with no face cream, powder, lipstick . . .

"That's your funeral. What on earth made you forget it?"

"I don't know. I was sure I had it, but . . ."

"They'll have to send it on."

I was furious. I was looking straight ahead. I wouldn't think about it. I concentrated on the ground. There was an old friend, the main railway line heading down to Dover, right underneath. I pressed the memory button. It's a pouring wet day thirty years ago. I'm in an SE5, ferrying it to France. It's 1918. The Hun has broken through. The C.O. has called for volunteers. I just happen to be at Brooklands on another job and here I am at 100 feet, glued to that railway line down to Dover, turning out over the gray sea, rain pelting on the windscreen, nearly running into the Calais cliffs, hopping over to the road, on to Marquise, and putting down the SE5 intact. "Where the hell have you dropped from?" "Brooklands. Here are the log books." I was back in town for dinner. It had been quite a day . . .

"It would save time if we turned back now."

"No."

Of course, inside I knew I should have to turn back. But I wasn't ready to admit it. Going back offended my sense of style. We'd planned, organized, worked up to this climax, and now . . .

"We'll discuss it at Lympne."

The wretched case might be anywhere: at the airfield, in the car, back at the house. It might take hours to find it. We'd just have to call from Lympne. But that might be tricky too. I particularly didn't want to hang about there. We were only just through the war, still rationed—not only for food, but for currency. All the authorities would allow me to fly across Europe was £10 for France, £10 for Italy, and £10 for Greece. It was ridiculous. At least two stops in each country—landing fees, meals, hotels: it simply couldn't be done on a tenner. So, neatly tucked up in the padding at the back of my seat was an envelope containing 250 pound notes. But we'd have to clear customs at Lympne. Go through all the "usual formalities." Might that include searching the aircraft? I didn't want there to be time for it. So the plan was to drop in, say we were making a dash for Paris, get briefed, sign out and push off smartly. And now . . . ? We'd have to hang around, phone, land—not once, but twice. Everyone would be alerted. They'd search the plane, and we'd finish up not in Joburg but in the jug. It really was the end . . .

However, we put down, did our phoning, located the precious case and arranged for my son to meet me at the airfield at Reading. Then, leaving Olga to ogle the customs boys, I took off again. Back to square one.

·

To me, there is nothing like the cockpit of an airplane. You are flying. One of the most wonderful of human achievements is in your hands. You are monarch of all you survey. Nobody can intrude on your solitude—or couldn't then; today, ground control is always barking at your heels, but in those days you could think your own thoughts, dream your own dreams, in serene isolation from all earthly cares, and, it seemed, grow wiser for your detachment.

It was an hour back to Reading and another to return to Lympne. Keeping half an eye on the world below, the Kentish hopfields sliding by underneath and the murk of London ahead, I still had time to ponder, to recap all the extraordinary decisions of the last few months.

My wife and I were not flying to southern Africa for pleasure. There was much more to it than that. We were pioneers, the spearhead of a project so important, not just to us but to the future, that it set us apart, made us "special," dedicated to a strange hope in which we fervently and wholeheartedly believed.

Now, in the sobriety of old age, the whole episode seems incredible, an adolescent fantasy that only very naïve, very credulous people could have undertaken. In fact, it seems as if for a period a whole group of us were hypnotized, under a spell—a spell woven by one man, an altruist, an idealist, enthusiastic for a new Teaching which was destined to change the world.

This man was John Bennett. He was in many ways exceptional. At home in the teachings of many religions—Islamic, Buddhist, Hindu—and with a wide knowledge of languages, he was at the same time a physicist and mathematician engaged in research on the relationship between gravity and magnetism and, besides this, such an authority on coal and coal derivatives that his expertise had earned him a prominent place on the Coal Board. In addition he was an inspired cook, a fine chessplayer, and a man of endearing charm and—when he chose to turn it on—compulsive charisma.

I give these impressions of John Bennett as I knew him to make it clear that he was no ordinary man, even if he was in some ways a volatile one. His adventures into the esoteric world led him along varied paths, but he was always sincere, a lifelong searcher in the labyrinth of religious truth. Since this is, for those who seriously undertake it, a voyage without harbor, we may question the ways he took but never the genuine impulses that prompted him. However all that may be, to him I owe the priceless gift of an introduction to the Teaching of Gurdjieff.

This Teaching, which had mesmerized a small group of quite serious people, was no weird eccentricity designed to attract "candidates for lunatic asylums," but a profound and comprehensive new model of the Universe and man's place in it which had an unmistakable ring of truth. It was, to us, a sort of revelation, opening enticing vistas. At the same time it stood the old ways of thought on their heads, often by arranging established facts in an unexpected pattern. If you were open to change and ready to accept that there was another way of thinking, another vision of reality, it became more comprehensive and convincing than any teaching that had gone before. At the same time, Bennett told us that, unique and revolutionary as this Teaching was, it was only a fragment—all he could remember of a whole that had been lost. Whether this was so or not didn't much matter to us. We felt we had been given enough spiritual food to last us a lifetime.

The source from which all this flowed was an extraordinary man, a Greek called Gurdjieff—of whom nobody had ever heard. We gathered that he had died during the war and, worse still, his only pupil, P. D. Ouspensky, philosopher and scientist, was also dead. The core of the Teaching had thus been lost, and Bennett, who had studied with Ouspensky for some years, alone remained. As this work seemed to him—and to all of us—a sacred trust, his main preoccupation was how to preserve and pass on the Teaching. It was his responsibility. He was the sole survivor.

In 1946 I was forty-eight years old. The Second World War was just over, leaving me disillusioned and dejected by the blind useless waste of it all—and more, by the evident determination of those running our so-called civilization to prepare for another war as quickly as possible. The new Teaching that I had met in that year seemed to me then—and still seems to me now—a light in the deepening canyon of disaster towards which we were heading, and I lent myself wholeheartedly to the daring and exciting idea that John Bennett proposed.

Like me, he felt that another war was inevitable, but he went further. He had convinced himself, and soon convinced us, that not only was another war coming but that it must come *within the next three years.* This alarming and fateful conclusion, as I remember it, did not faze us in the least. We swallowed it whole. Our reaction was that if this Teaching was to be saved, a safe deposit must be established where there was some chance of its survival in the holocaust that would soon overtake Western Europe. Long, serious discussions were held on ways and means: where to go, whom to send, what to look for, how to organize the project, and so on. After examining the possibilities of Canada, Australia and New Zealand, it was finally decided that somewhere in southern Africa was the best place. None of us knew Africa or had ever been there, but that did not matter. Scouts would be sent out, a site would be chosen, ground would be purchased and a pastoral community set up. Pioneers would establish all this, other members of the group would follow, various crafts would be added, and it would all grow into a self-supporting community sustained by the principles of the work in which we all believed and would thus be preserved for the world to come.

The starry-eyed idealism of all this never entered our heads. It seemed to us a natural and commonsense solution to a difficult problem. It was also an exciting adventure to begin a new way of life in an unknown country, with all the challenges that might bring. This suited me very well. I did think the values of Western civilization were being fatally eroded. The belief that "more" was a solution to anything seemed to me a dreadful fallacy. In the new young countries there could be hope. Another way of life could begin. After all, why not? I had come through two world wars; they had both disrupted my life. I had no job, no career to return to, nobody wanted me or needed me. My new and beautiful young wife seemed to fall in with all these ideas with remarkable adaptability. So, just to put panache on the whole thing, I decided to buy an airplane to quarter the terrain and find our future home. All the plans were now complete and here I was flying the airplane, bound—once we had got that damn make-up case aboard—for Paris, Milan, Athens and all points south.

I put down at Reading, my son handed me up the precious make-up case, and without stopping the engines, I turned and took off again for Lympne.

Setting out on a 6,000-mile transcontinental flight means an awful lot of bumf: your "ship's papers," giving you ownership; your airworthiness certificate, without which you aren't allowed to fly the plane; your pilot's license; your insurance—all this has to be in apple-pie order, since you're constantly crossing frontiers. In addition to medical certificates showing you have had the necessary jabs, and passports, you have to carry a lot of detailed information about the airfields on your route and the approaches to them. The sky wasn't as crowded in 1947 as it is today, but there were already lanes for commercial aircraft, prescribed heights at which they had to fly, approach zones, landing procedures, and so on. Much of this wouldn't worry us, since we wouldn't be using the big commercial airfields and crowded centers, but we had to have the lot in case of emergencies.

In all this the Royal Aero Club had been of invaluable help. They were a mine of information about everything on our route. Planning the route itself had been quite an exercise. It was easy enough in Europe, but once you got to Africa there weren't many places where you could put down in an emergency. Although we had a range, with full tanks, of about 800 miles, we didn't want to exceed 400-mile hops so as to have a bit of reserve if we ran into bad weather or lost our way.

Of course, we had a suitcase full of maps. Indeed, the question of navigation had aroused quite a lot of alarm and despondency. We ought to have a navigator, they said; it would be much better. When I told them that I was the navigator, it didn't seem to impress them. For we were already leaving behind the days when the pilot was automatically the navigator. He got to his desintation because he could fly and read a map. He flew, as we used to say, "by the seat of his pants." Nowadays beams, beacons and radar have superseded maps. The modern crews usually fly high above the overcast and never bother to look at the ground until they are approaching their destination. But I was an "old-style" pilot. The ground told me where I was. If the weather was bad, I didn't proceed. I had hundreds of hours' experience of getting from point to point. All I needed was a map—what more did I need? I had my eyes, hadn't I?

And that brought up the question of communication. What radio was I carrying? None. But you must have it, they argued. What about your approach? Airfields are pretty crowded. You must warn control of your arrival, take your turn on the runway—you might cause a fatal pile-up if you cut in ahead of some airliner. Why should I do anything so stupid? Couldn't I see the damn thing coming? And at night? I didn't intend to fly at night. I'd done hundreds of hours at night, trundling around airfields, doing circuits and bumps, training young hopefuls in damp, windy weather with a ceiling of 500 feet—no thanks, I intended to sleep at night.

But, the helpful people insisted, there were places up the Nile, dangerous places, where a forced landing might be fatal if you had no means of telling people where you were. Did I want to die of thirst? If I hadn't got a radio I must have an escort, and how was I going to fix that? So finally I gave in. I couldn't carry a proper radio, but I might be able to squeeze in a short-range radiotelephone. Well—they shook their heads—perhaps that was better than nothing.

Fitting that radiophone was quite a saga in itself. To start with, I couldn't really afford it.

"Try the Americans," said a chap who knew the ropes. "They're dumping all their radio equipment, burying it."

"Burying it? You're joking."

"No. They're burying all their radio sets—spares, stores, everything. What are they to do with it now that the war's over? Nobody wants the stuff. It would cost thousands to ship it all back to the States, and what would they do with it there? Simply find some other hole to bury it in. So they've bulldozed out a nice big one at Hendon and they're just dumping it."

I couldn't believe it. However, when I got in touch with

the people who were doing the dumping it turned out to be quite true. Had they a small radiotelephone they could let me have, if they'd no further use for it?

"Sure. Come on over and help yourself."

So I went along and helped myself to a complete radiotelephone set: microphone, earphones, amplifier, the lot. But the Gemini was a very small aircraft, so the components had to be installed right in the nose. You couldn't get at it to tune it in the air; you had to pre-tune it on the ground, and that never worked. At airfield after airfield, as I came in I would religiously call up, give my number and request permission to land. Dead silence. Nobody ever answered. It was a complete waste of time.

I put down at Lympne. Actually the delay turned out to be to our advantage. My wife had done her stuff, everyone seemed anxious to get us away quickly. In half an hour we were cleared. Nobody even bothered to look at the aircraft. We were off.

•

The cloud was thickening up from the south as we headed out over the gray sea. The Channel is a moody piece of water and that afternoon it looked sad. But we were soon over it, headed south; the cloud was ten-tenths at 4,000 feet and we pushed on beneath it. It was about a two-hour flight. We should just drop into Paris nicely before dark. My spirits rose. After all, it was a bit of an adventure. Not many people fly themselves down to southern Africa in their own private plane, and I looked forward to the challenge of it. The engines were dead steady. I had the throttles so nicely adjusted that there was practically no interference beat; when the trim was properly set she would fly "hands off." The cabin was snug and comfortable, my wife, now freed from all cosmetic anxiety, was sitting relaxed and composed by my side, we had a date in Paris which promised to be interesting, and all was well.

That afternoon our "interesting date" was far more important to me than the spiritual adventure on which we were embarked. And this contradiction between the different sides of people stood right at the heart of this teaching to which we adhered. We always think of ourselves as whole, individual, solid, like pieces of sculpture, always the same. We have our moods, of course; everybody does. But essentially we have a core, a self, an "I" with which we face the vicissitudes of life. But here was a typical example of the way our new teaching stood old ideas on their heads. Not so, said Gurdjieff. We have thousands of "I's." We change from moment to moment. We are blown from contradiction to contradiction by every puff in the wind of circumstance. There is nothing permanent about us.

This is such a ridiculous idea that nobody can take it seriously. But in fact, if we try to face what is going on inside us every day, we see something very different from the idea we have always taken for granted. A procession of quite different people—each calling himself "I," of course—troops through our waking hours, each separate, with a separate set of values, separate ideas of right and

wrong, like and dislike, good and evil, and all these different people—often quite hostile or unknown to each other
—take charge, and do what they like with the whole of us
until the next "I" turns up. It is not a case of Jekyll and
Hyde, but of a thousand Jekylls and a thousand Hydes,
each ruling the roost in turn. "Our name is legion for we
are many." While one "I" is up, none of the others is there
at all. Angry, we are all anger. Sad, all sadness. Loving, all
love. And we skip from one to the other, blind to the
contradiction.

So now I had quite lost sight of the great enterprise on
which we were embarked. Where was my irritation at a
piece of forgotten luggage? The experienced pilot flying
to Paris had disappeared to be replaced by a sexy "I" very
intrigued at the prospect of meeting a stranger my wife
had picked up while having tea at the Ritz a week before.
It was an unusual thing for her to have done. What was the
idea? All I got was an enigmatic smile . . . Well, I thought,
the Lord Krishna is often depicted playing pranks with the
maidens he met in the woods. I had seen those exquisite
miniatures and, after all, my wife was half Burmese and
this girl was said to be a beauty from Thailand . . . Anything
could happen. Why not?

We met up with Zaza, as she called herself, for supper.
She was indeed a stunning girl: but clearly her calling
would have presented no enigma to the panel of *What's
My Line?* She evidently considered our company an excuse for an evening off and consumed vast quantities of
frogs' legs with garlic, which made her lethal at three

paces. But her anecdotes, very salty and frank, of men and their pranks, were certainly not miniatures and soon had us roaring with laughter. So it did turn out to be an "interesting evening" after all and we were quite sorry to leave behind this savor of traditional Paris when we took off for Nice the next morning.

2

To Nice

OUR DIRECT ROUTE SOUTH from Paris toward Italy and Greece would have taken us across Switzerland, but the peaks there were well above our ceiling. Mont Blanc is over 15,000 feet high, and we could not get above twelve. We might have been able to weave ourselves through the valleys with the mountains towering above us on either side, but supposing we took the wrong turn, so to speak, and got into a cul-de-sac? It couldn't be done, even on a clear day. On an overcast day it was suicide. So we would have to go around.

Going around meant flying south to Marseilles, skirting

the coast to Nice and Genoa, and then turning north into the Lombardy plain and Milan. The first leg of this was easy. We would just fly south, pick up the Loire some seventy miles south of Paris, and follow this on to a place called Le Coteau. From there Lyons was less than fifty miles ahead on the left. We should probably see it from the Loire, and nipping over to it we couldn't very well miss the Rhône, which would lead us down to the coast. If it was a clear day, we should see the Massif Central on our right and the Alps on our left. It was all perfectly straightforward. The distance was about 400 miles—three and a half hours in the air. Marignane airfield was large and clearly sited on the flats near Marseilles. We should just about make it for lunch.

There was broken cloud at 5,000 feet that morning, and a fresh southeasterly breeze made the air turbulent. So to escape from being thrown about, we climbed through the cloud, thinking it would break up as we ran south into warmer air. We could still see patches of earth through the cloud gaps, but these grew more and more infrequent. Soon we were soaring above an endless field of white. The sun shone out of a blue sky, and although the right thing would have been to come down again underneath it all and read ourselves carefully along our track, I made the wrong decision and decided to carry on south on a compass course. After all, we were bound to reach the Med sooner or later. We couldn't very well miss the sea.

But mysterious things go on in the air of which a pilot flying without any navigational aids can have absolutely no idea. Winds shift, reverse direction, increase in speed and height, and once above that innocent field of white, you have no idea where these unseen currents may be taking you.

I'd had a very good lesson in all this when I was learning to fly for the second time, in 1942. It was a miserable day. The cloud base was less than 500 feet over Upavon. My instructor looked at it. "Let's get up through this and practice a spot of aerobatics." We wedged ourselves into the Avro Tutor and took off through the overcast. It was only a few hundred feet thick, and once through it, we were up into a glorious winter morning. A sheet of misty white stretched before us to the horizon.

"We'd better put down a marker," my instructor shouted through the intercom. "Never know where you'll drift to."

I couldn't think what he meant. Put down a marker! In the sky? It was nuts. He then proceeded to carry out a maneuver I have never seen any other pilot execute. We shut off and came down right onto the flat top of the cloud sheet until we were flying through the misty stuff of its upper surface. Then he threw the old Tutor into a vertical bank and we careered round and round in a tight "split-arse" turn, with the lower wing tip furrowing through the cloud. After four or five turns he yelled, "That'll fix it," and we climbed away.

Looking down, I saw we'd carved a perfect circle in the cloud. I suppose it's a thing which would only work on a very still morning. After half an hour's exhilarating slow rolls we located our marker easily and came down through it. It had drifted a few miles from the airfield but we were home in ten minutes. Without it we might have come out miles away.

But there was no question of markers that morning. I'd set the compass grid to 160° and was holding a steady course. The sun shone, the engines were fine, and we felt that wonderful godlike loneliness you get flying high and solitary, between a dome of blue and the Elysian fields of white. The poor people grubbing about on the earth somewhere below were all in shadow, while we were up here in a marvelous cupola of sun.

All the same, after three hours of it I began to wonder. No sign of a break in the cloud, no mountain peaks sticking up through it—and if we were on course, there should have been. Over on our left from this height we should at least have seen Mont Blanc, but there was no sign of it, and I began to get just a shade anxious. On our right, again if we were on course, lay the Massif Central, the peaks of the Auvergne—they only reach 6,000 feet and we were at 9,000, well clear of them. We'd gone into cloud at 5,000 feet and it might easily be 1,000 feet thick, so they would be buried in it. But wherever they were and wherever we were, nothing whatever showed. Nothing but this endless glistening plain.

Well, no use worrying. I held on for another hour on the same course—four hours. If there was no wind, we ought to be over the sea by now. If there was a following wind, we might be well out to sea. If there was a headwind, we might be . . . anywhere. I had no idea where the wind was, nor its strength. Might as well face it, we were lost.

You may not believe me, but I once saw a qualified navigator of an R.A.F. bomber crew absolutely lost 10,000 feet over England on a cloudless summer morning! It was a couple of years before the Second World War. We were flying down from Scotland toward Oxford. It was such a perfect day that the whole crew was in holiday mood. The aircraft was pointing roughly south, and there was well over an hour to go before we were due to arrive, when suddenly the captain called to his navigator on the intercom, "Chris, how are we doing? Where are we now?"

Chris was deep in a thriller, miles away. He snatched up a map and came up behind the pilot to have a dekko.

Now, England has a landscape like no other country on earth. It's so compact, so webbed with roads and railways running in every direction, that from a height it's so full of feature as to be featureless. No great mountain ranges, no large rivers, no obvious landmarks that you can't miss. There it is, cut into millions of meadows, "fold, fallow and plough," copses, lanes, villages—it's such a tightly woven pattern that nothing much sticks out. Chris was evidently flummoxed. He used the old trick of pointing the map the way we were going, and began to try and pick up the landmarks while the rest of the crew tittered, and the captain frowned—for I was doing a series of articles for a big London daily, and he saw the R.A.F. being written up as a bunch of nitwits. Of course Chris soon got it sorted out —we were over Ripon, that was York on the left, Leeds and Bradford coming up through the smog—but for a few moments I had that curious feeling of knowing I was somewhere but not exactly where.

That morning our situation was a little more dicey; we would have to let down through cloud. The trouble about that is, from above you can see where the top of the layer is, but you can't have any idea where the bottom is. This is the way even experienced pilots sometimes get caught and seemingly inexplicably fly into mountainsides, in spite of all their navigational aids. We had no aids, and I had a rooted aversion to mountainsides at close quarters. Still, nothing else to do . . . I cut back the throttles, and we began a slow power descent.

The cloud, which had looked so solid and smooth, began to lose its clear-cut surface as we came down over it. At 7,500 feet it was a swirling golden web of mist, and then we were into the cold gray blanket. The engines just ticking over, everything seemed to go silent. We were sinking through this ghostly fog: nothing above, nothing below or around us—an absolutely featureless, horizonless world. There is no situation for a pilot as nerve-racking as this. How deep is the cloud? Does it go right down to the deck? If there is any chance of a mountainside or even a hillside about, he will be into it before he can possibly see it. Visibility isn't fifty yards. Besides, he's on instruments: having no horizon, he must trust his false-horizon indicator, hold it level, watch his speed, his compass, his height, his rate of descent. His eyes flick from one dial to the other, for steady instrument flying depends on keeping all these components in balance. The modern aircraft captain has an automatic pilot to do all this for him, but we had no such help. Besides, I am not a skilled pilot on instruments. I can do it, of course, but I had none of the experience of those bomber pilots who could hold course, speed and height, flying blind through cloud for hours on end.

I never make a descent through cloud as an airline passenger without remembering that morning. Of course, the captain has called the tower and been told the height of the cloud base; he can see the airfield below on his radar; it's all absolutely safe. But all the same, I'm always relieved when I first see the dark shadow of earth coming into focus through the last veils of cloud—and we are still well above the deck.

We were down to 7,000 feet now, and still no break in the cloud. The peaks of the Massif Central, Mont Dore and Plomb du Cantal topped 6,000 feet, and if by some dreadful bit of bad luck we had drifted east, and came down on top of them, it was curtains. I put on some flap and reduced the speed to 50 m.p.h., as low as I dared. It might just give us a chance if we came out on a steep hillside. Slowly the altimeter began to sink—6·8, 6·5, 6·3 . . . My heart was pounding. Would the damn cloud never thin out? 5·9 . . . 5·8 . . . There! There was a patch—something . . . A shadow. Was it sea? It ought to have been sea, miles below . . . No, it was earth. Steep. Either side mountains rose. Ahead was a clear gorge—a valley vista, a horizon. The relief was terrific. Up flaps, full throttle. We shot away toward the distant sunshine.

A headwind must have held us back and drifted us west. We'd come down in the Massif Central—no doubt about it. Where we were exactly didn't matter, as long as we could see a way out. We headed southeast, steadied up at 5,000 feet, and began anxiously to look for landmarks. No sign of the sea. But at last we picked up the Rhône and all was well. Still, it was another hour before we sighted Marignane and put down after five hours in the air.

During the war, Transport Command had set up a network of staging posts all around the Med. They were mainly for ferry pilots taking new aircraft up to the line or bringing back others for overhaul or repair. Marignane had been such a staging post, and in 1947 it was still nothing much more than a few huts, a radio mast and a runway. There were no facilities for peacetime aircraft, or for passengers. No canteen, no snack bar, no signs of any place we could stay for the night. It was a gray, deserted place—and then it began to rain.

As we stood about in the doorway of Flying Control, chewing the rag about our trip with the staff on duty, nearby stood a young man, evidently a pilot, getting himself cleared. He told us he owned a Messerschmitt, and when we said who we were and where we were going, and how we had almost no money, having spent most of our precious £10 in Paris, he suddenly said, "Come on with me to Nice. I live there. I'll put you up."

"Are you going in this?" It was pouring.

"Why not? I know the way perfectly, just follow me."

It was friendly and generous and a bit of very good luck,

for instinctively I trusted the man. Pilots are pretty consci-
entious about their trade. He wouldn't have made the
suggestion in such poor weather if he wasn't perfectly
confident. So we got the tanks filled up, cleared for Nice,
and within half an hour we were airborne again.

I soon saw that Monsieur Chapeau—for that was what
the young man called himself—was a very skilled pilot.
Something about the confident way he handled the Messerschmitt was reassuring. The rain that burst on the windscreen came from a series of showers, but as we climbed,
Monsieur Chapeau skillfully kept in the dry valleys between them and we were soon high above the great canyons of cloud, seeing the earth from time to time, sliding
past as if at the bottom of an aerial well.

The distance from Marignane to Nice is only about 100
miles—under an hour's flying—but Monsieur Chapeau did
not follow the coast; he cut across "the hump," leaving
Toulon, St. Tropez and the Côte d'Azur on our right. We
couldn't see it anyway. It was masked by rain. But we
knew we were in Provence. From time to time, Cézanne
country with all its yellows and umbers slid into view for
a moment and then was blotted out again by ragged cloud.

The Messerschmitt was a single-engine job, but it was 50
m.p.h. faster than we were. Monsieur Chapeau forged
ahead. Soon he was just a speck of black on the white face
of the next cloud. But then he swung off in a tight curve,
circled back to us, came up astern, passed us with a wave,
gave us the course by his own direction and swept ahead
again. Such is the companionship of the sky. Again and

again he repeated this maneuver. We were in good hands.

Although it was only a short hop, I have exhilarating memories of that flight. We were, it seems now, almost always threading our way through mountains of cloud. Though they were close and towered white above us on either side, we ourselves were in clear air. Only occasional flurries of rain starred out on the windscreen. I had quite given up trying to keep tabs on our course, having after a few minutes grown to trust our guide completely as he returned again and again, shepherding us through the maze of cotton wool. It was comradely—and at the same time it was heroic. There is something godlike about the sweeping arc of an aircraft; tilted, veering, purposeful, and yet so lonely, so small, against the gorges of the sky.

Such memories as these belong to that very small group of pilots who flew before radio aids were compulsory, before ground control constantly nudged the pilot to maintain his course and height, monitoring his every moment, anxious for his safety, calling on him to report his position, tethering him with invisible cords to the earth from which he has escaped. The commercial airline pilot has skills of the highest order but I don't think he has much fun. Only a few amateurs with their private planes can revel in flying for flying's sake. One can't imagine a pair of jumbo jets playing follow the leader among the clouds as we did that day. The passengers would be sick and the pilot would lose his license. Flying, perhaps man's most remarkable—and certainly his most romantic—achievement, has become prosaic, positively pedestrian in outlook; nothing more than a quick way of getting from A to B.

How lucky, then, we were to be flying an aircraft you could throw about, as light as a sheet of paper in a breeze, so much part of you that you felt its every movement, alive as you were, sensitive to every change of mood and reflecting a joy, more free than any other, of just being alive!

After about forty minutes of this, Monsieur Chapeau swayed his wings from side to side as a sign for us to watch him, then he stood the Messerschmitt on its nose and shot down like a diving fish right into the cloud beneath him. It is, I think, the most wonderful moment in flying. Push the stick forward, flick up your tail and down you go. The speed screamed up, in a flash we were into the cloud; a second later it opened, and there was the sea. We were dropping like a stone. Waves were breaking in a long line of foam against the coast, and parallel to it, hardly fifty yards inshore, was the broad black asphalt road of the Nice runway. We eased out of the dive, watched Monsieur Chapeau land, dropped our undercarriage, felt the slight jar as the wheels dropped in the down position, followed him in, kicking the rudder lightly to counteract the cross-wind, and rolled into the sheds.

•

Nice, because of the tales of the "battle of flowers," its legendary gaiety and beauty, had always beckoned me as one of the high spots of the Côte d'Azur. Its reality on a

wet October afternoon was depressing. It was like being
shown a derelict house after reading the glowing writeups
in the agent's brochure. Deserted streets, closed shops,
empty roads; it felt like a ghost town, and we were glad
when Monsieur Chapeau turned his car up into the hills
and stopped at his pretty villa high above the sea.

There he introduced us to his wife, a timid creature,
who evidently didn't expect him (and certainly not us).
There was an awkward atmosphere and soon we began to
feel ill at ease. The skilled pilot on a friendly impulse had
invited us to his home, but that "I" had quite gone now,
and had been replaced by an almost surly, defensive man,
stuck with unwanted guests. However, he poured us
drinks and we sat about for some time making conversation, but it was difficult. Monsieur Chapeau evaded all
inquiries about his profession, or indeed about anything
personal. His little wife was plainly terrified of him, and he
dismissed her to cook some supper as one might a servant.
Having gratefully accepted his hospitality, we tried to do
our best to be good guests, but it was heavy going. How,
I asked him, had he got his Messerschmitt?

"I bought it."

"That was a bit of luck—I mean, a German aircraft so
soon after the war. It must have been difficult."

"Not really."

"I've never seen the type before. Was it a communica-
tions aircraft or something . . . ?"

"I imagine so."

"Do you fly much?"

"When I feel like it."

"Not much fun at this time of year."

"No."

"Where do you fly to?"

"Anywhere I fancy."

"And you, madame," I turned to his wife, who had just come back into the room. "Do you enjoy flying with your husband?"

She blushed and stammered something, but he cut in.

"She does not like flying. She is sick."

It didn't go very well. Monsieur Chapeau was a good pilot but he wasn't a good host. My wife seemed to get on with him more easily, so I excused myself and went into our room to study maps. Later she joined me. "That's a tricky one," was all she said. After an indifferent supper, we retired early.

Next morning at breakfast, the conversation happened to turn to money, and I said that my wife and I had a joint banking account. It was a good idea. Probably he did the same thing? He was outraged.

"*I?* Share money with my wife? Certainly not! Certainly not! Why, she would waste it, run up bills, indulge in all sorts of extravagances . . . I would never dream of doing such a stupid thing."

"But," I persisted, "I take it you trust her, and if you trust her . . ."

"Ah, m'sieu." He looked at me pityingly. "You are English but I am French."

While he went to get the car his wife came out onto the

front steps, plucked a rosebud and gave it to me. "May you have a safe journey," she smiled. At that moment Monsieur Chapeau returned.

"And have you no rose for your husband?" he asked sarcastically.

"Why yes, of course. But you said you did not like them." She flushed, and picked another.

He took it, looked at it, and flicked it away onto the path. "No, I do not like them," he said, "but I like to be offered them."

He drove us to the town, indicated the place where the bus left for the airfield, and curtly said goodbye.

What had we done to make him behave so churlishly? We stood there in the rain with £4 in our pockets, a filthy day, and obviously no chance of getting away. A friendly gendarme put us onto a cheap boardinghouse; we had a sandwich lunch and found a bistro for supper; but all day Monsieur Chapeau was the topic of our conversation.

"He obviously didn't like us," I said. "Why?"

"I think he was jealous of you. Jealous of us for having a better sort of relationship than he had."

"Do you think she was his wife?"

"Of course not."

"I was sorry for her."

"She made a dead set at you."

"D'you know what I think," I paused. "I think he was a smuggler."

"A smuggler?"

"Yes. Fast aircraft. Nips down to Spain, Algeria, Morocco, Tangier. Comes back with anything that's small and valuable: watches, dope, diamonds, currency. That's why he was so cagey about his flying."

"He made quite a pass at me—and she came in in the middle of it."

"No! What did you do?"

"Nothing. What could I do? She quickly went out again."

"Now I see why we were invited."

"Of course, darling. You are so naïve."

Next morning, the weather looked a bit better, good enough for us to get away. We had to get away in fact. We'd only four francs left.

3

To Milan

WHEN WE HAD FOUND OURSELVES in Nice, we naturally
thought of going back to the Gemini to milk our private
bank. But finally we decided not to risk it because of an
officious little weasel of a man in the French customs.

"Your aircraft is in bond, Mr. Lewis—you understand?"
he barked at us, "—until you take off."

Now he went through all the suitcases with quite unnecessary thoroughness and took hours stamping our passports and papers.

"Now, currency, m'sieu. How many francs are you taking out of the country?"

I showed him our four francs, telling him that we had only been allowed £10 for France.

"And where did you change your money?"

"In Paris."

"Where, in Paris?"

"At our hotel."

He exploded. "Hotels have no right to change money. Money is to be changed at a bank. To change money at hotels is against the law. That is black market money. What rate did they give you?"

I named the rate. It was well above the official bank rate. He was white with anger.

"Give me the name of the hotel."

When in Paris before the war, I always used to stay in a little hotel in the Rue de Rivoli. They knew me well, so on arrival we had gone straight there, only to find that the place had been commandeered by the Americans as an officers' club. We went on to another hotel; but that gave me my chance. I gave him the name of the hotel where we *hadn't* stayed. He wrote it down venomously, with obvious pleasure. "We will deal with them. I assure you, m'sieu, we will deal with them."

I was chuckling inside all day. I'd fooled the little bastard. We collected our papers, humped our suitcases out to the Gemini, and quickly took off in case he'd phoned the hotel. It was the only bright spot of our stay in Nice. Never have I been more glad to get away from a place.

Just beyond the frontier with Italy, the Maritime Alps march forward to the sea. We flew along over the water,

parallel to them, climbing hard. Well before they reach
Genoa, their 10,000-foot peaks had dwindled down to mere
hills, four to five thousand feet high. Now the cloud was
lifting all the time; we were well clear, and turned north-
east over the tail of the mountains toward the Lombardy
plain.

It was a sort of discovery to find this flat fertile country
beyond the mountains, and we marveled at the view. Beneath were the silver ribbons of the tributaries to the Po;
to the northwest the mists of Turin; ahead, Milan, with the
great ranges of the Alps proper filling the northern horizon. The sun was through and the whole prospect, washed
fresh after the rain, was sparkling in the sun as if the world
had been re-created anew for us that morning.

It was in fact being re-created anew for us every day, all
the time, but we didn't see it. Today I regret, more than
anything else, how much I have missed in the glorious
wonderful life that has been granted me. I see how I have,
so to speak, slept through it, for I am being bombarded by
life all the time and I firmly believe it is all recorded in my
computers. But it is as if I had just left them switched on,
so to speak, without noticing what was going into them. So
everything is forgotten, or at least only half-remembered,
out of focus. Most of my life seems to have been lived this
way. If I could really keep tabs on what happens, I should
see the facts, the way things are *at the moment,* that is,
"reality." But I don't do this. When I "remember," it is
almost always distorted, blurred, put together afterwards,

an *idea* of what happened, not the reality itself. And I have been born, educated, conditioned all through my life to consider this secondhand way of living as normal.

So when I met the teaching of Gurdjieff and was told that we live our lives in illusion, that we are all asleep, I had no difficulty at all in accepting it. The implications, of course, are so shattering that most people have to repudiate them as nonsense. But what about those moments of deep joy or sorrow in which we see life afresh? We remember them vividly as quite different from the way we usually are. The possibility of trying to return to such states never occurs to us. It seems like a revelation, an illumination, a moment of clairvoyance. But teaching in all religions aims to show us ways to regain this state, which is reality, and to live there as long as we can.

Certainly we both had a moment of wonder that morning at the miracle of just being alive, and it seemed confirmation of all we had been taught. It was, incidentally, a bonus, for this leg of our flight was a detour. From Nice we could quite well have flown east-southeast toward Florence, but we had a special reason for doubling back: it was to say goodbye to the villa I had built on the Lago Maggiore, which had been my home on and off for almost twenty years.

It was Sunday, and when we landed at the small airfield south of Milan, we found an amateur flying gala in progress. Dozens of private aircraft stood on the tarmac and the whole place was seething with people. It was all noisy, gay and carefree, bubbling with Italian festive vitality, so we bribed a taxi driver to ditch his fare and take us to town. There, we got a train to the lake.

The Rupi—my villa in Italy—was the most wonderful gift ever made to me. It was in my thirty-first year that Charles Ricketts, my patron and dear friend, had come trotting into his studio one morning with a check in his hand. "My dear boy," he had said, "here's a check. Take it and buy that bit of ground of yours in Italy." When I protested that I couldn't accept such a sum of money, he waved me aside. "Take it, take it, dear boy," he said. And then, after a pause, "Don't let's be sentimental, but it would be something to remember me by." Sadly, he never saw the place; overtaken by misfortune and grief, he died (in his sleep) without ever visiting it. But I remember him and always shall, not only for this but for the cornucopia of care and love he poured over me that lasted even after his death.

The ground on which the villa stood was situated outside the little village of Arolo on the east bank of the Lago Maggiore. Eight acres of terraces and precipices, a quarter of a mile of waterfront, it looked across to the Alps over four miles of water. From the moment I first saw it, I fell in love with it, and it became mine for £350. Over twenty years, on slender means, I managed to clear it, plant it, and build a tiny house on it. Little by little it grew into a sort of secret paradise that bewitched everyone who came there. I always knew it was a millionaire's place (it is now owned by one), and that day, en route for Africa, I was leaving it again as I had so many times before, not knowing when I should come back.

We got out of the train at Varese and took a taxi through the twenty miles of narrow lanes—for that side of the lake had not then been developed—to reach Arolo. The village gave us its usual big-hearted greeting; willing hands took our suitcases and walked us by the narrow cobbled track to the old iron gates, along the garden path beneath the precipice, and at last to the little secret house perched over the water.

If places retain an aura from the life that has been lived in them—and I believe they do—then the Rupi had been lavishly endowed. It had never known death, or sorrow, or any unhappiness. It had always been a refuge of peace and simplicity, the setting for many idyllic affairs, a retreat for writing, a bolt-hole of escape in '38–39 when Europe's lease of peace was fast running out. Now unchanged, untouched by six years of war, it was still there waiting, serene, lovely and faithful, to welcome us back.

The soil at the Rupi was poor. Many things did not thrive. But we had a hedge of forsythia that in early spring shone right across the lake. Wistaria clambered high up onto the walls of rock and cascaded down in a torrent of blossom. In one natural amphitheater in the garden, we built a semicircle of steps, rising to a pergola at the summit where a niche was cut out of the rock. In this stood the bronze bust of Charles Ricketts, which he had left me in his will. The pergola, dripping with wistaria, shaded those bronze eyes which had never in life seen the beauty of the gift he had made me.

I had been at some pains to devise a plaque to be placed below the niche, and I remember the consternation of the stonemason in Varese, faced for the first time in his life with the need to twist his chisel around English words. They read:

CHARLES RICKETTS
gave this rocky precipice
to Cecil Lewis who here made a garden,
so to commemorate in beauty
a great artist
and a noble and generous friend.

The Rupi has, alas, changed hands since then, but so far, bust and plaque have been left where I placed them, undisturbed. I hope they always may.*

•

We stayed a week in the little place. Every day, Rena could be heard pattering along the path, come to cook those mouth-watering risottos and tagliatelles as she had

*I have already commemorated Charles Ricketts in my autobiography, *Never Look Back*, and in a volume of his letters and diaries, *Self Portrait*, published in 1939. Not only a Royal Academician, painter, lithographer and exquisite draughtsman, he also designed outstandingly for the theater. His work for the first presentation of Shaw's *Saint Joan* was brilliant, and all his theater drawings are now the property of the National Art-Collections Fund. But beyond all this professional attainment, he was a generous, lovable human being, with interests and erudition in many fields of art. He was indeed, as William Rothenstein once described him, "a truly civilized man."

done for twenty years. Adolfo, who had loved the place and built it for me, had made it grow from a wilderness of woods and brambles to a wonderful garden. Now he dropped in every day with a gift of fish or grapes, or a cake his wife had baked in the communal oven, to bring us up to date on the village gossip, to make plans or settle accounts, and always to entertain by his shrewd peasant wit and his endless fund of stories.

"Did you notice that new villa just outside Leggiuno, the one with the green gate?"

"Yes. Who built it?"

"That old rascal Giorgio, the priest at Santa Caterina." (Santa Caterina hung on a precipice over the water, a few miles down the coast. It had been a monastery complete with a saint's tomb, miraculously preserved from destruction under a huge overhanging rock, and was a popular place of pilgrimage during the tourist season.)

"No! Where did he get the money?"

Adolfo smiled that knowing smile of his. "You know how people throw their soldi down through the railing around the tomb? Well, it was his job to pick them up. Yes . . . religiously, every evening. He's been doing it for twenty years . . ."

"So?"

"Well, they were offerings made to God. So to be on the safe side, this *lazzarone,* when he collected them, just threw them up in the air toward Him. Anything He wanted would remain up. What came down, He obviously didn't want . . . Yes. It's a nice little house . . ."

It was, I suppose, in prescient mood that the night before we left we gave a party for the entire village. Over the tennis-court—the only one in the world where if you hit a ball out you had to retrieve it by boat—Adolfo slung a wire, with a wheel and a seat below it. On this the children took aerial rides, shooting down from the high ground at one end, screaming with excitement. Everyone was there: the masons and carpenters, gardeners and laborers who had helped to build the place, with their wives and relations. There were lights in the trees, tables on the little terrace loaded with salami and cheese and olives and sticky cakes. There was wine, lots of good red wine they had trodden with their own feet. Some of the older ones, as the fumes began to do their noble work, began to sing the simple songs of the village—

> Papa non vuole
> Mama in meno
> Come faremo
> Fare l'amor'?

All the while, their womenfolk tried to hush them, it not being quite right, as guests of the *signore,* to let yourself go. At length, after many *buona notte*s and *dormi bene*s, the last footsteps faded, to leave the midnight peace of lapping water.

I did not then know (mercifully) that it was the last night I should ever spend at that house which Adolfo and I had built together. In the long years since I could easily have returned to it, but somehow I did not wish to find it changed, "improved" by other hands. Better to keep it fresh in memory as I left it . . .

Losing the Rupi, I lost not only the gift of a dear friend, but a whole passage in the golden years of youth. Perhaps the very loss sharpens the memory. All we hold, in any case, we hold on lease from life. Although other lives now live through it, nothing can touch what I gave to it and what it gave to me.

Adolfo and Rena came down with us to Milan, and we took them up for a flip in the Gemini high above the city. Neither of them had ever flown before, and the excitement of it masked the sadness of our parting. Next morning we took off for Brindisi.

4

To Athens

SOMEHOW, IT WAS NOT UNTIL WE CLIMBED away from Milan that I began to realize the extent of the flight before us. Because Italy had been for so many years my second home, I had not felt, up to that moment, that we had really "left." But now our way lay unknown before us, and as if to drive it home, we rose into a perfect morning—and couldn't see a thing!

October mists have a romantic association for most of us, but their effect in the air, if you are flying into the morning sun as we were, is to blot out the whole landscape ahead in a golden haze. That morning, it was like flying over fog, so thick was the blanket. The earth must be there, there was nothing between us and it, and yet I had no idea where it was or where we were. Expecting to map-read our course by the railway line that runs down to Bologna, I hadn't bothered to set a compass course. Now I quickly studied the map, spun the grid to 100°, and settled down to it. A bit over an hour would bring us out somewhere on the Adriatic, and surely we should see that.

"It's perfectly clear behind."

It was Olga who had happened to look over her shoulder, to see below our tail the whole vista of northern Italy as clear as a bell. Of course, I should have realized it. Against the sun an opaque haze of gold; with the sun, the clarity of water. I gave her the map.

"See if you can pick up anything. You should be able to spot Pavia, Piacenza, and the railway line towards Parma."

She knelt on the seat and, for quite some time, carefully compared the map with the landscape.

"I think I've got Pavia," she said finally, "and there's a road, quite straight, coming from it right under our tail."

"Must be the autostrada."

"It's absolutely glorious behind."

"I wish it was in front."

"Nothing to worry about, sweetie. We're okay."

With this reassurance, we pressed on, checking from time to time by "retrospective navigation." We had taken off a bit after eight; about four hours should see us down to Brindisi. No difficulty about navigation there. We only had to keep the east coast of Italy under our port wing, and as the sun rose higher the haze would thin out and disappear. Already after an hour we began to see the ground below; another hour and it was as perfect a day as you could wish. There on our left was the blue of the Adriatic about two miles below; to our right, the crinkled valleys of the Apennines; ahead, the whole leg of Italy.

What a prospect! What a country! No other people had poured out such a torrent of creative art, century after century. The very names of their cities were inspiring: Verona, Venezia, Padua, Assisi, Siena, Perugia, Ravenna; they rang in the mind like trumpets, like the fluttering of triumphal pennants on some medieval pavilion—

> Open my heart and you will see
> Graved inside of it, "Italy."

So wrote Browning, and that morning, floating ghostly above it all, it seemed we were borne up by the almost palpable presence of long-dead masters: Leonardo, Michelangelo, Fra Angelico, Donatello, Tiepolo, Botticelli, Bellini; they had all lived, worked and died somewhere there beneath us, and we, mere passers-by, a little white buzz in the blue, were proud to salute that age when beauty cradled the sanctity of the spiritual life . . . And then there was the music! Donizetti, Verdi, the divine heartbreak of Puccini . . .

"Darling," said a voice at my side, "I think we should land now."

"Land?" I was miles away. "Where?"

"Oh, anywhere."

I didn't quite take it in. "Are you crazy?"

"No, but . . ."

"There isn't anywhere to land."

"I must spend a penny."

"Spend a penny?" It really was the limit. Nothing but mountains and sea two miles below. Spend a penny!

"We can't land."

"Then what am I going to do?"

"Can't you hold on? Forget it?"

"I'm afraid I can't."

It certainly was a dilemma, and somehow, in the way one overlooks obvious things, we'd never thought about it. After all, four hours—anybody ought to be able to hold out for four hours . . . Then I had an idea.

"What about your hot water bottle?"

"Hot water bottle?"

The idea had evidently never occurred to her. It hadn't occurred to me until that moment.

"Won't it corrode or something?"

"Probably. But you can rinse it out with T.C.P. at Brindisi."

"I'm sure it'll ruin it."

"Well—too bad."

It took some time to locate it in the suitcase, and by this time I'd seen the funny side of it all and was laughing.

"It's all very well for you to laugh. It would be easy for you."

"Luckily it's got a funnel."

From the care she took to screw up the top, the thing might have contained holy water. She leaned it carefully, stopper up, against the back seat.

"You ought to say 'For this relief, much thanks.' "

"It was very awkward."

But my mind was already slipping away, back to the conundrum of Italy below us. I had often thought about it. The mystery of the Middle Ages. What sort of life had those people lived? The ordinary people. They had their wars, their feuds, their social and domestic problems like everyone else. But at least half their lives, it seems, were genuinely devoted to quite another life, the religious life, a consolation from the sorrows of the life they lived. There could not have been this outpouring of great art—cathedrals, churches, monasteries, palaces, and all the sculpture and pictures and decorations that overflowed from them —without a deep longing and love of almighty God. The ambition to live an honest God-fearing life that would lead to personal salvation was evidently real, and they raised monuments around them everywhere to remind them of it.

But their daily life, the care of their bodies, was, by comparison, negligible. It didn't seem to interest them. Personal and public hygiene was non-existent. People lived and died in clothes they had worn for years. The body was a mystery, and their ideas of the working of it an ignorant fantasy. Michelangelo risked prison for daring to dissect a corpse. Leonardo may have understood the function of the heart and the circulation of the blood, but this is not certain. (Half his diaries have been lost.) In short, daily life was largely focused on spiritual hopes of heaven or fears of hell, and the physical, imperfect, sick and often ill-treated body was accepted for what it was.

And today? Exactly the opposite: an offhand, superior attitude to anything concerning the spiritual life, but a seemingly insatiable appetite and ambition to delve deeper and deeper into every detail of the workings of the body. Life, it seems, is always lopsided, swinging to opposites, to extremes, which in turn arise from ignorance and fear. We deeply need a more harmonious approach. Doctors who are not just medicine men, but physicians for the body and the soul, who realize that physical and spiritual needs cannot be separated and that the health of the flesh and of the spirit is indivisible.

The day will come when our moral, spiritual and mental health will become as much a burning question of the day as heart surgery or genetic engineering. There will be a sudden awakening to the fact that our attitude to spiritual matters is childlike, primitive, shot through with lies, make-believe, fairy tales; not really a serious subject to be taken seriously by mature people. When this happens all our present ideas about such things will be swept away, and a new vision of reality will emerge.

"Isn't it about time we saw the Trulli?" said my wife.

"Soon now."

I looked forward to showing them to her.

The Trulli lie in a small stretch of country between Bari and Brindisi, back in the hills—and there is nothing like them anywhere in the world. In 1943, when I was commanding a staging post in Sicily, I managed to scrounge a Hurricane for my personal use. One day, flying in formation with my son, who was taking a new plane back to his squadron on the Adriatic, I happened to glance below and saw some very odd round houses. After we parted company, on my way back I dropped lower to look more closely. Curious round houses were dotted all over the place among the vineyards. They stood in groups of four or five, four or five circular pointed roofs, clustering up out of the common retaining wall, for all the world like a cruet. It was very strange. I had no idea what they could be.

It wasn't until some time later that I was able to explore this magical, hidden bit of Italy. There is something fey, pixilated, about the little places. They stand like fairy castles, on the summits of small hills, surrounded by their vines and the glorious, chocolate-red, ploughed earth, so rich it looks as if you could eat it. Nobody seems to know who invented the Trulli, or from what root they spring. Their circular roofs, pointed like a dunce's cap, are not tiled but made of flat stones piled one above the other, each drawn back a little from the one below, so gradually a tall cone is built which, crowned by a round stone ball, makes it look as if the whole thing had been impaled by some gigantic pin. The Cross of Lorraine is often whitewashed on this roof, and inside, it is plastered to a smooth round funnel. Tiny fairytale windows pierce the walls and low doors join the adjacent rooms so that, as you walk from room to room, you are always under these tiny domes. My son and I spent most of a happy day exploring these wonderful little places, spotlessly clean and cared for, and toward evening happened to visit one where quite a crowd of people were gathered. It was *vendemmia,* and relatives from nearby towns had come out to help get in the harvest. The sweet fumes of the grapes had already made them a little merry, and now they welcomed us warmly, and the father of the household, aided by his son, began to lift a huge round stone from the center of the floor. Into the hole, while we watched, fascinated, he lowered a jug on a piece of string and pulled it up overflowing with amber-colored wine. This was the way to keep last year's wine, he told us, cool in a cistern below ground. Would we care to try some? So, drinking from the jug, we did. So did everybody else. It was very good. We all agreed it was very good and we must certainly have some more, so we did, and soon the dark southern girls were rolling their eyes at us (and other things beneath their jumpers), and dear old Bacchus was exhorting us to indulge in those improprieties which, in this part of the world where tempers are fiery and jealousies extreme, are only a step away from high words and knives. So, somewhat unsteadily, we made for our jeep and ran down to the coast to dine at a roofless castle above the sea.

Now, losing height, we came down and turned inland above the Trulli, and I banked the Gemini this way and that to show my wife these little gems of southern Italy which I had so often told her of. It wasn't as good as seeing them from the ground, but it was something.

Ten minutes later we touched down at Brindisi.

•

The temporary wartime airfield at Brindisi, like all the others, was abandoned soon after the War. Our engines ran on ordinary car gasoline, but there was none at the field, so someone had to go into town and get it. This wasted two and a half hours, while we fumed about, finding nothing to eat but a rough salami sandwich, and impatiently awaiting the arrival of our fuel. When at last it came we filled up quickly and took off, for it was another four hours on to Athens and only with good luck should we make it before dark.

We headed out across the Otranto straits, leaving the slim heel of Italy on our right. Before us lay a good sixty miles of water. Pilots of small aircraft are apt to get a little tension in the solar plexus at the thought of engine failure over the sea. But all was well that glorious afternoon. The water was sparkling blue and soon we saw the offshore islands north of Corfu, floating like lumps of pumice-stone far below us. We left them to port and reached the coast of mainland Greece somewhere near Preveza. Inland towered the mighty ranges of the Pindus, cockade after cockade of dun rock, upflung against the sky. Ahead, the low marshy estuaries of Missolonghi. Offshore, on our right, lay the hundred islands of the Inland Sea protected by the famous Ionian chain: Levkas, Cephalonia, Ithaca and

Zante; one of the most inspiring seascapes in the world.

By now the sun was massing his evening magnificence to lay a benediction on the day. His rays, reflected upwards, turned the Ionian into a glittering targe of molten silver, on which the islands lay like encrustations of ebony, beckoning and forbidding. Above, tremendous rafts of cloud hid the sun, but shooting up from below came shafts of light, quiver after quiver of refulgent gold, till the whole western heaven was suffused like one glittering, airy monstrance, tremendous, austere, and somehow sacred. We sat there, high above it all, I remember, full of exhilaration, gazing with a sort of heady joy at the beauty of the world, privileged to hold for a fleeting moment ringside seats on the very lip of the Creation.

Before the magic faded, we had turned east and plugged on along the Gulf of Corinth, a sleeve of dark water. It was a long stretch, longer than I had dared to admit to myself. The light was going. On either side the mountains towered, shutting in the sea. It was too dark to find Delphi, and Parnassus was no more than a heavy menace in the northern gloom. But I found I was still holding the memory of that sunset, a sunset such as I had never seen in my life. In some special way it had touched my essence, and I should never forget it.

Essence! It was one of the key words in this teaching we were now flying so far to preserve. It opened up a new idea in the concept of man; an idea you would not find in any other teaching.

From the first moment a new life is conceived, its individuality is indelibly stamped into every atom of its being. This newborn creature is all essence and it is unique; there has never been anything like it. But this new life is also born with a marvelous battery of computers, whose business and nature it is to record everything perceived. Life sets the tapes spinning and all our perceptions are registered: perceptions of thought, perceptions of feeling, of habit, behavior, and so on. They are all vividly recorded. This is the stuff of memory. But everybody has such a set of computers, and all eagerly impress their ideas on those of the new arrival; and so quite early a sort of covering or mask is built up, woven from all these impressions which smother and even supplant the newborn essence which lies within it. It is as if someone made you a present of a bottle of spirit, gift-wrapped. All you can see is the outside. You may like it, or dislike it, but in either case it gives you no idea of the nature of what lies within.

Now these are the facts. They are not theories or hypotheses about human behavior. They are before us, and anybody can verify them at any and every moment. We receive millions of impressions throughout our lives, and we have a marvelous facility to stir them all up: to add, distort, overlook, and synthesize what we receive, and so create a mishmash that we genuinely think of as our own —our own thoughts, our own beliefs, our own convictions and so on. But in fact they are not our own. They are nothing but associations—the combined reflections of what our computers have recorded. Memories, ideas, actions, reactions; all, without exception, are secondhand, old stuff on file, read-outs of what has been fed in.

Meanwhile, inside the giftwrapping is the hidden essence, unable most of the time to manifest itself through this aggressive, active, busy covering—the personality with which we face the world. To begin to see this is to see the very nature of that "sleep" I spoke of earlier. And to verify it by our own observation is to face a terrifying state of affairs. Life as we live it is no more than a mix-up of secondhand ideas, a make-believe reality, an endless tissue of lies from which there is no escape until we begin to listen to the whispers of essence, that is, of our real selves, and wake up. Essence does not lie, knows our needs and what is necessary for our lives. But at the same time it is not some super-self. Essence can be greedy, ambitious, feckless, generous, but it is genuinely *us*—not some pretentious façade we have built up out of the dreams of how we would like to be. But how to find the essence, how to discriminate between what is really us and what is our wrapping, this is the beginning of a struggle toward reality, to another life.

Before we reached the Corinth canal, the light had almost gone. Optimistically, I had thought of Athens as just beyond the cut. In fact it is a good fifty miles further. Before we reached the Bay of Salamis, the earth below began to be pinpointed with lights. Ahead lay Athens. How it had changed! Ten thousand streets were aglitter. In three years, the 1944 darkness had quite gone. Among it at first I could not make out where the runway was, although I knew it well from those exciting days when the

ELAS rebels rose against us, and we were all within an ace of being pushed into the sea . . .

No use fooling ourselves! We were caught out, in for a night landing—and we weren't prepared for it. Our Gemini was not equipped with searchlights in the wings. It was an expense I had cut out, not intending to make night landings. However, just in case, we had purchased an Aldis lamp. This gave a wonderful beam and, hand-held, could be poked through the cockpit window. When finally I made out the two insignificant strings of lights marking the runway, I cut back the engines and we started to come down. Olga was busy fishing out the Aldis, unwinding the flex, plugging it in, sliding back the cockpit window, ready to poke out the light and switch it on when I told her to. Now we were on finals, flaps and undercart down, fifty feet above the runway, coming in from the east. We had bags of room and had just judged it nicely, for after all, I'd made hundreds of night landings and I knew my stuff.

"Okay, switch on." There was a pause. "Switch it on."

"It is on."

"It isn't on. God Almighty."

Landing an aircraft is a matter of seconds. There's no time to argue or change your mind. It was an instantaneous adjustment. No lights—then we'd use the runway lights. I kicked the rudder to slide over nearer to the left-hand line, cut the engines, held her off, and we were down with a rumble on the tarmac.

"Nice work, darling, that was a beauty."

"What's wrong with that damned light?"

"Look." She shined it toward me. The bulb emitted a faint glow.

"God, the twits! They must have given us a 24-volt bulb for our 12-volt battery! Never mind, we're down. Let's get out of here."

Some instinct made me turn off the runway onto the grass. I've always wondered why, for the logical thing would have been to carry on down the runway to the exit. We'd called the tower on approach, but as usual, with our wretched R.T., no answer. Now we were off onto the grass and not a moment too soon, for almost immediately a DC6 loomed up and thundered past, *landing in the opposite direction!* Well, a miss is as good as a mile. We taxied in and found Mitsos, an old Greek wartime colleague, now in charge of the airport. Delighted to see us, he took charge of the Gemini, rushed us through customs, found us a taxi, and we were off to town. It had been quite a day.

5

To Tobruk

WE STAYED A WEEK in Athens. Close friends from the difficult days of 1944 put us up, and took some pride in showing us how the city had got on its feet again. We did all the usual things—dined at tavernas, visited the Acropolis by moonlight, goofed at the Mycenae gold in the museum, and bought a sponge. It was exhilarating to be back in Greece. The vitality, the good humor, the hospitality— all these I remembered from those stirring days in 1944. More than anything else, what set Greece apart was the marvelous quality of her light. So clear, so pure, so crystalline in its quality, you could very well believe, as her ancient philosophers had claimed, that through such skies you could see the gods and reach the very sources of truth.

Certainly on Liberation Day in 1944, when I flew into Greece from Cairo, the morning was sparkling with promise and hope. As we approached Attica across the Cyclades, every island—as if to celebrate—had a garland of cloud above it, and the reflections in the still water of the islands and cloud islands wove a mazy, insubstantial pattern between blue sky and sea. Then there was Athens ahead, a pile of white cubes tumbled out on the bare brown earth. Hymettus swung up on our right, there was the Acropolis, that must be the Piraeus. We were all very excited, for there had been quite a build-up to this day. Greece was one of the oldest British allies, and the chaps on board our Dakota were all specialists of one sort or another, come to help in the rehabilitation of the country after four years of German occupation. Few of them had ever seen Greece before, but the romantic tradition of her art and architecture had fired their imaginations. We touched down and began to get our bearings.

Up in the city that night there was a deep murmur of joy welling up through the crowded streets. They had been lit for the first time in years. Every house flew a flag, the beautiful blue and white flag of Greece, and an endless river of people streamed through the city. The hated Nazis had gone. You couldn't walk a yard without being accosted by people of all ages who, with strange words and gestures of delight, clapped you on the back, took your arm, offered you a drink and gave you that accolade of warmth and welcome which it is not easy to forget.

But gradually another mood seemed to seep into the city. We had been warned of rival political groups before we came, but these warnings had been largely disregarded. Greece, after all, was an old friend, and we had come to help her to forget the miseries of war and set her on her feet again. It was impossible there should be any difficulty. But as the days went by, it appeared there was a very active aggressive group who did not want our help, except on their own terms, which were to take over the country. Groups of partisans began to appear in the streets —young men and girls, armed with revolvers, bandoliers of ammunition and big sharp knives. They were an impressive lot of ruffians, and one day, as we watched a parade of four thousand of them marching through the city, it looked as if we might be in for trouble.

It was trouble partly of our own making. Ever since the Allies had got back into Italy, active help had been sent to the Greek partisans to harass the Germans and run them out of Greece. Liaison officers had been dropped by parachute, lavishly equipped with gold sovereigns, to be followed later by our aircraft landings, loaded with weapons and ammunition. But the extent of the rejection of the pre-war Greek government, and the well-organized Communist infiltration, was not realized. The arms and ammunition provided to fight the Germans were largely diverted to become the armament of the partisans. The Germans left Greece practically unmolested, and a horde of well-armed young freedom fighters descended on Athens.

General Scobie, the G.O.C. Greece, had of course refused the partisans' demands. When things had settled down, when the roads and railways had been reopened, bridges rebuilt, when the country began to be more or less normal, then elections could be held, and Greece, the founder of democracy, could decide her own destiny. It was unthinkable after four years of war against dictatorship that the country should be taken over by a Communist mob, which these ruffians represented.

The personnel sent to rehabilitate Greece were not fighting men. Most of them, including ourselves, were technicians, mere civilians in uniform, quite untrained in warfare. So finally, when the partisans decided to act, there was very little to stop them. They quickly overran the Piraeus: no ships could dock or deliver supplies. They looted and commandeered at will. They got hold of a 15-pounder and began taking pot shots at the Grande Bretagne Hotel, where the British headquarters was situated. It wasn't safe to go about in the streets, for at any door you might find a woman standing legs apart, while the spout of a rifle, aimed by her partisan husband lying prone behind her, took pot shots at you. We all had strict instructions not to molest any "friendly" Greeks. But who were friendly Greeks? The partisan just put his rifle up the chimney, clapped on a Homburg hat, and cheerfully came out to greet you. He was a "friendly" Greek.

Day by day the situation got worse, but it was not until the entire headquarters staff of the R.A.F. in Greece, and two-thirds of my own unit, had been blown out of their hotels at dawn, and taken prisoner by hordes of partisans, that the seriousness of the uprising began to be apparent to Whitehall. On Christmas Day, Churchill flew out and came under fire at the British Embassy. Alexander followed and ordered in an airborne division.

"The arrival of that Airborne Division" (I quote from my notes of the time) "was the most exciting episode in my R.A.F. career. Top-secret signals began to pour in: 'Forty Liberators arriving! . . . Twenty Wellingtons arriving! Fifty Dakotas arriving!' For the first three days the ETA of these aircraft was identical. They all turned up precisely at 11:00 a.m. I have never seen anything like it. The sky was thick with aircraft.

"All normal procedures were scrapped. The boys played it by eye. Stacked up one behind the other, wheels and flaps down, it was nothing to see six on finals at the same time. An 'A.C. plonk' at the head of the runway fired volleys of red lights to space them out, but the pilots took absolutely no notice whatever of these red lights. One burst tire or one faulty landing and there would have been a monumental pile-up. But it was a magnificent display of airmanship. Coming in hard on each other's tails, so that before one aircraft was off the runway the next had touched down, they rolled in perfectly and followed the jeep with its checkered flag to their parking position. An army lorry slid alongside, the aircraft was off-loaded, and the pilot taxied onto a prepared take-off area.

"At this pitch of over one hundred aircraft arriving simultaneously the airlift lasted three days. Then we got it organized. Arrival times were spaced out and the heat was off. But even so, they were terrific days. Organizing scratch meals for four hundred aircrew was a strain on our resources. One night when the weather clamped in Italy and a hundred crews could not return was the climax. They thought they might all be shot up before morning. This amused us greatly—for we were used to the conditions and couldn't believe we were in much danger— which was far from the truth."

It took a month to winkle the rebels out of Athens, and it was spring before Attica was normal. Those bitter winter months, lived mostly on iron rations, gave us quite an insight into the Greek character. They were basically individualists. They could never agree long enough to organize or be organized. They didn't understand maintenance or upkeep. They were a brave people, tempered by poverty and centuries of Turkish oppression. But person to person they were your equal. You saw it in their independence, in their frank greetings, in their generosity, their humor, their friendship. Yet they were unpredictable, irresponsible and fatally self-destructive. You could never rely on them.

This little-known skirmish with the Greek partisans had made an exciting end to my personal war, and I bowed out of the R.A.F., for the second time, the following May. Now, only two years later, I was back, renewing a sheaf of memories of those days: the golden tracers from our MTBs pounding into ELAS strongpoints at Castella; waiting for two hours in the freezing afternoon on Christmas Eve for Churchill to come out of his aircraft; driving at night down from Psychico drenched with the scent of honeysuckle; the cheer that went up from the men after we officers had served their Christmas dinner, when I told them that we had news their mates were safe; Greek girls decked out in their national costumes on Independence Day; the hum of the tiller in the little cutter that friends had lent me, as we ran home across the Bay of Phaleron; the day I was given a week's special leave and sent home to surprise my wife. Now she was here to see the place where I had known all this. All the anxiety of the earlier days had gone and we basked in clear pleasure.

·

But we could not linger. We had a date in Nairobi and had to go. So we said our goodbyes and went down to Hassani, ran the engines carefully and got a weather forecast. It told us there were storms over the central Mediterranean, but promised good weather over Africa. I hesitated. Storms at the most dangerous part of the long crossing were something I would have preferred to avoid.

"Take no notice of the forecast," said Mitsos cheerfully. "It's always wrong. Usually it's just the opposite of what they say. How can they know what the weather is like in the central Mediterranean? They haven't been there."

I laughed. He was probably right. We decided to give it a whirl. We would get down to Crete anyway. If it looked dicey there, we could always land. So we took off and climbed through broken cloud.

Of course, it was foolhardy to be making the long sea-crossing at all. It was only sixty miles from Sicily to Castel Benito, and that would have been the prudent route to take. But Olga wanted to see Greece, and it was the most direct route, so we decided to risk it.

But all the same, I was, frankly, nervous. 400 miles to Tobruk. That was a lot of sea. It was 200 to Crete, but there were islands; stepping-stone islands, most of the way. But beyond that there were another 200, empty, all sea. Halfway across that, with our ceiling, there was an area of no return where, if we had engine failure, we could neither get back nor reach Africa. We would be done for it. But so far, anyway, the engines were fine. We were soon well above cloud, which blanketed the sea and the islands. Far ahead we could see the long black hump of the Cretan peaks sticking up through it. When they came abeam, below our left wing tip, it would be time to set a careful compass course for Tobruk. The cloud ended south of Crete as if it had been cut off with a knife. Mitsos was right. The weather was the exact opposite of the forecast. The central Mediterranean was basking in perfect sunlight. But there was no land on the far horizon to beckon us or give us hope—nothing but an immense blue disc of water. Below our 100-mile horizon, the maps told us, was Africa. But you need faith to believe what you cannot see, and the little cockpit became a lonely place. I remember vividly my feelings that morning. The challenge, the fear, the moment of decision. Why were we doing it? It seemed there were special moments when you did not so much take decisions as were swept into them.

It had been the same when I first came into contact with the teaching of Gurdjieff. I had been given a book, and was reading a chapter about the Law of Three. It told me that what we normally think of as the Holy Trinity was in fact a way of naming one of the two fundamental primordial laws of the Universe. It was sacred not for the mystical, half-understood, "religious" reasons that were usually given, but because it participated, indeed created, every event, every happening in life. Life was triadic and proceeded by the coming together of three forces: one proposing, one denying, one reconciling. From the spinning of the galaxies to the creation of the snowflake the same laws operated. It was God's thumbprint on the Universe.

Half-consciously that morning, I had turned the page. On the next there was nothing but an equilateral triangle. At the apex stood an "equals" sign, at the bottom left a minus, at the bottom right a plus. Nothing else. The triangle didn't explain anything. It didn't ask to be understood. It was just there: the "I AM" of the Universe.

I was transfixed by it. I didn't know why, and it didn't matter. There was an absolute certainty that this was truth.

"Is anything the matter?" said my wife, looking up from her book at the other side of the fire. "Your face looks quite different."

Well, that was certainly one of those special moments when "an angel plucks you by the hair." I didn't decide at that moment to study the Gurdjieff teaching. I was, so to speak, swept into it by the power of the experience.

And here we were, committed to this long hop over the sea; swept into it without making a definite decision, "shall we or shall we not go?"

"Now I wish we had those life jackets," said Olga. So did I. Of course, it was absolutely ridiculous to be making such a crossing without life jackets. But back in London, plotting our course, it hadn't seemed worthwhile carrying them just for one hop. They were extra weight, they wouldn't be much help in the desert, so we'd made light of it ("what matter if the diver has no snowshoes?"); we'd take our chance. Well, we had taken it, and now it seemed very foolhardy.

Soon we were entering the zone of no return where, if our engines failed, we were bound to come down in the sea. We both knew it. We'd often discussed it. But now we didn't speak, we just waited, listening acutely to the engines, noting the oil pressure, checking the compass, and staring, staring, staring at the southern horizon as if by looking hard we would see land sooner or bring it nearer. After what seemed an eternal half hour, we were theoretically through the danger, provided we maintained our height, of course. But now—what was that ahead?

It was a huge wall of cloud, filling the sky before us, reaching up far above our puny 12,000 feet, and solid right down to the water. Fine weather over Africa! It had been wrong again, that forecast. That cloud meant rain, rain over Africa! The desert was having one of its rare torrential storms, and here we were, arriving bang in the middle of it.

We plugged on, hoping it might clear further south, or be less solid than it looked, but as we came closer, we saw that we were out of luck. We couldn't risk running straight into that cloud; it might be a hundred miles across. We should have to fly under it, even if it meant doing the last hour right down on the deck. Well, nothing to be done. I cut back the motors and started our descent.

We hoped the cloud base might be at least 5,000 feet above the water, but as we came lower we saw it wasn't. It wasn't 4,000, or 3,000, and we were down to 2,000 feet before we could see underneath it, through driving strings of rain. But now the sea began to change color. It was no longer deep blue but paling out to a sickly emerald. That meant shallow water. The coast must be near. Yes, there it was! Thank God. A narrow thread of yellow at the limit of our vision. My, it was good to see that coast! The rain was pelting down, hammering on the big windscreen, but we hardly gave it a thought. And what was that, just over there on our right? Masts! A ship—the harbor of Tobruk! We'd hit it right on the button! It might be a triumph of navigation, but it was also a fantastic bit of luck. We shot in across the scarred remains of the town to land at El Adem. We had reached Africa.

6

To Cairo

WE LOST NO TIME in getting away from El Adem. The storm had cleared, the sun was out, so, after grabbing a sandwich and a cup of very bad coffee, we took off for Cairo. It lay 450 miles to the east, and we were determined this time to get in before dark. There was no navigation to worry about, we couldn't very well miss our way, we had only to follow the coast to Alexandria and then turn inland to the capital.

But it was deadly monotonous. On our left, nothing but sea. On our right, nothing but sand. Featureless wastes of desert dotted with scrub and occasional black dots—the

carcasses of burnt-out tanks—were all that remained of
one of the most famous battlegrounds of history. It was
here—only five years before—that the tides of the Allied
fortunes had turned. Not the beginning of the end,
Churchill had warned, but the end of the beginning. Rom-
mel's brilliant advance had been slowed, halted, and
finally rolled back. But only just in time. And now, of all
these great battles, of all the heroism, courage, skill and
effort, not a sign remained.

> My name is Ozymandias, king of kings:
> Look on my works, ye Mighty, and despair!

It might be Montgomery's epitaph, for surely there never
had been a campaign where the fruits of victory had left
less mark on the ground it had been fought through. Not
a cross, not a tree, no sign of death or life. Not even a
burnt-out truck on the lonely Via Balbo.

It was a bitter comment on war and depressed us as we
droned on over it, hour after hour. The desert grew to
seem monstrous, a useless freak of nature. How had it been
formed? What gigantic forces had combined to create
such a nothingness?

In my childhood we were taught that the Sahara had
once been a seabed, later raised by some shrinking or
squeezing of the earth's crust. In parts of the Western
Desert this was true: but in the Sahara it was not. There
were no sea shells or remains of them there. It was all rock,
powdered rock, inert, lifeless, dead. Could there have

been periods when great gales blew, endlessly, for centuries? Had whole mountain ranges crumbled under this pitiless erosion, been ground to dust, and been carried on the wind to drift and settle and blot out an area bigger than Europe? In our comparatively peaceful period of the earth's evolution, we cannot imagine the scale and ferocity of the cataclysms that poured molten mountains and ground out the ocean beds. Compared with that, a few centuries of wind would be very small beer. It seems the only way to account for the sands.

But beneath them—it has now been discovered—lies fertile earth. The desert could blossom like a rose—if only the sand were gone. Indeed, a pre-sand civilization flourished here. Remarkable rock drawings have been discovered by teams of archaeologists, exploring districts so remote they had to have basic supplies flown in by helicopter. At a place called Tassily, a whole life that had once been lived has been found, drawn on the rocks: horses, giraffes, deer, crocodiles, ostriches, fish, wildfowl; herdsmen guarding their flocks, hunters throwing their spears, strange blindfolded giants sitting in judgment—a whole way of life, scenes observed and loved, confided to the rocks, perhaps ten thousand years ago. And now rediscovered, they reveal a life once lived, every bit as wonderful —and brief—as ours, when all the world seemed young.

Well, it was older now, the miles of sand insisted. And the day was drawing to a close before we began to see signs of habitation along the coast. They seemed to thicken up towards the eastern horizon. This must be the beginning of Alexandria. We turned southeast to cut a corner and began to look for the outskirts of Cairo. But it was further than we thought—our destination always seemed further than we thought—and behind us a typical desert sunset was building up, a naked, fiery ball glared over the sand, and a broad swathe of orange stretched on either side of it, lying heavily on the earth like the sediment of a hot day. I knew that, once the sun had gone, it would be dark in ten minutes, for the nearer you get to the equator the shorter the twilight, so somewhat anxiously I was trying to calculate the sun's height above the horizon and to set this against the distance we still had to cover. But as I didn't know either with any exactitude it wasn't much good. All I could do was to put the nose down and begin to lose height, hoping that with a bit of extra speed we might just make it.

Then there were the Pyramids ahead, their western flanks shining gold. Even from our height they looked huge. From the ground, by moonlight (as I had once seen them), they towered black above me, as if their peaks held up the sky. Their mere size was enough to evoke awe, even worship. They were perhaps the most extraordinary structures ever raised by man. They filled the sky. You could not escape them.

I do not believe great civilizations erect monuments on such a scale for mere vainglory. The monuments are above mere vanity and power. Built by some Pharaoh they must have been, but the more we ponder the stark simplicity of their shape, the more the mathematical precision of it takes on the authority of law. The pyramid is stating something, stating it categorically, without any possibility of contradiction or doubt. This is the truth: truth for yesterday, today, and all the days to come.

In a curious and unexpected way, it reinforced that moment I had experienced myself at seeing the Law of Three in triangle form by my own fireside. Here was indeed a huge reminder of it, given stature and solidity by its roots going back into the distant past. Of all the ancient civilizations known to man, none remotely approaches that of Egypt in magnificence and duration. Such a tradition of government does not just "happen" by the seesaw of political expediency or the scourge of despotism. It springs from a long experience of the principles of wise government which in turn are rooted in religious convictions. A civilization which endures for 4,000 years must have been constantly renewed by a profound and penetrating understanding of the nature of man and God.

The pyramid is a universal symbol. Just as the church bell is a summons, a call to remind men of their need to live a righteous and godfearing life, so the pyramid, towering above men, reminds them of the constant presence of their gods. It lifts their eyes to the apex, to the divine source of life from which all proceeds, and shows how the descending orders of life proliferate, always in the same harmonious proportion, down to the base on which they live. The weight of the whole creation rests on this base. It is here we live and that is why the earth is a very heavy and complicated place. But progressively as the spirit struggles upwards the weight and complexities of life grow less, and always, to whatever height a man may come, there are the same noble proportions, the same four faces of life to be kept in harmony, which, rightly proportioned, may make the whole man. The pyramid is not some fabulous monstrosity—a dragon or a unicorn—but a symbol which proclaims the wonder and mystery of the Universe itself.

We left them that evening on our right, their flanks burnished as they had been for a million evenings before by the last red rays of the sunset, and pushed on to land at Heliopolis, on the last drops of light.

7

To Waði Halfa

BEFORE LANDING we had heard there was a serious outbreak of cholera in Egypt. Although we had been inoculated against it, B.O.A.C. officials (who were looking after us) advised us not to risk visiting the city as we had planned to do, but to get away south, out of the infected area, as quickly as possible. Accordingly, after spending the night in a bedroom so huge that a double bed in it looked like a stamp on a postcard, we were taken straight back to the airfield and took off for Luxor.

From the air, you quickly get a general impression of the country you are flying over. Egypt is very strange.

Except for the Delta and the irrigated strip along the banks of the Nile, not a blade of grass grows, not a tree, no road, nothing. And through this waste flows the country's artery, the river Nile, which does not receive a single tributary for the last 1,000 miles of its course! There it flows, lonely and somehow defiant, holding back the greedy sand. It has done so since men can remember. But it seems to warn you—and the warning does not take long to sink in—better stick close to me if you hope to survive. The rest of this land is not to be trifled with.

The desert south of the Delta is intimidating country. It is a maze of jagged ravines, steep, narrow gullies, once evidently eroded by water but now as dead as the sands that silted up the dried watercourses of their base. Even at 10,000 feet it seems to warn you to be on guard against this dreadful menace which, since prehistoric times, has stretched a blanket over Africa from the Atlantic to the Euphrates.

Yet, paradoxically, right in the heart of it had flourished the most enduring civilization in recorded history. Other empires, Roman, Spanish, British, lasted 500 years, but Egypt stood immovable and magnificent for 4,000 years or more. What is the secret? What had they understood about the conduct of life that had held the country together, and indeed increased its authority as the centuries rolled by?

It was a paradox within a paradox. In spite of great armies, great generals and constantly increasing conquests which established Egypt's dominion over the then-known world, the whole life of the nation, the skills, the effort, the enormous wealth, were focused not upon this life but upon life after death, life in the world to come!

An incomparable outpouring of monumental tombs and temples bears witness to these beliefs. But over the centuries, the fixation with this idea grew into a fantasy of rituals and a hierarchy of gods and lesser gods, guardians of the underworld and so on, which circumscribed and permeated every moment of life. Over all this stood an all-powerful priesthood which owed its place to the fact that, at least in the beginning, the direction of the whole country lay in the hands of Priest-Kings, worshipped as divine, as living gods.

It can be generally agreed that, from time to time, exceptional beings do appear on earth, whose bearing and authority are such that people conceive complete trust and respect for them, and are eager with reverence to carry out their orders. Many hope, during the lives of these men, that they will set up their spiritual authority on earth—it was indeed the temptation of Jesus—but as far as we know, none have succumbed to this temptation, insisting that their kingdom was "not of this world."

However, it is not impossible to imagine that some such Being took it as his task to see if it would be possible to create a kingdom on earth whose people could live whole and honorable lives because of the right discipline and direction of their inner life. In such a way, Priest-Kings could have arisen who really were human yet divine, and to whom was entrusted the government of the country.

Such men, setting up schools of pupils who were prepared to endure the rigorous disciplines necessary to reach higher levels of life, leading to compassion and impartiality, could have carried on the initial divine impulse of their founder to create a hierarchy of superior beings to whom reverence and obedience were owed because of their sacred lineage. Such was, perhaps, the only foundation on which a society such as Egypt's could have lasted so long, only to break down when the ruler's self-respect for his own honor and divine status finally died out.

"Visit Luxor if you like, Mr. Lewis, but you will not come back."

The officious young Egyptian who spoke these words sat, one leg on the table, idly swinging a fly-whisk. Dusty fez, greasy stained tunic, overbearing manner, the young man represented authority at Luxor airport.

"I hoped to visit the Valley of the Kings."

"Visit the Valley of the Kings if you like, Mr. Lewis, but you will not come back."

It was evidently his formula.

"We have cholera here. Bad cholera. Have you seen men die of cholera, Mr. Lewis?" I shook my head. "You would not like it, Mr. Lewis, you would not like it. Leave the airport and you will be infected—"

"But we have been inoculated."

He whirled the whisk around his head in the bare smelly room. "Infected," he went on, "and carry the disease with you to your next stop. That cannot be permitted. Well—what will you do?"

He was right, of course, but his brash officious manner

was quite uncalled for. He was taking it out on me for being English. It angered me. Suddenly I felt I wanted no part of him, or Luxor, or anything Egyptian. All I wanted was to get out of the damned country as soon as possible.

"I have no option," I said as quietly as I could. "I will leave at once."

"Give me your papers."

He made no move to take them from me. He just sat back, leg on table, glaring at me. I felt if he could cook up any excuse to thwart or delay me he would. I put down the papers on the desk and went out to give the news to my wife. It was extremely hot. She was standing talking to a young man in shorts, underneath the wing of an old Anson —an aircraft that had gone out of service in the R.A.F. at least seven years before. I had not noticed it when we came in.

"Hullo," I said. "What are you doing here with that old kite?"

"Trying to get cleared to Wadi Halfa."

"Where are you from?"

"U.K. We're ferrying on to Rhodesia."

"Bloody hot."

He nodded. "That bastard in there. We've been hanging around for four hours already."

"All these wogs are the same."

It was another two hours before our papers were returned to us. Two hours standing about in the blazing heat, nowhere to go, nothing to eat, we daren't touch the water. We wasted no time in climbing aboard. The cockpit was like an oven. The Anson still hadn't been cleared.

"See you in Wadi Halfa."

"Hope so. Cheerio, Mrs. Lewis."

He was a nice boy. Meeting a dish like Olga in that flyblown dump had made his day.

We climbed up gratefully into the cooler air. With our roof curtains drawn, we sat in shadow. At 10,000 feet it was bearable. We set course for Wadi Halfa.

But it was sad to have missed the glories of Luxor, because nearby, on the east bank of the Nile, was something I had wanted to visit all my life. Now it was just a patch of desert, no different from the rest of it, but once upon a time . . . it had been the symbol of the world's eternal hope.

> Ah, love! could you and I with Fate conspire
> To grasp this sorry Scheme of Things entire,
>   Would not we shatter it to bits—and then
> Remould it nearer to the Heart's Desire!

These famous lines catch at the heart of every lover, every poet, every dreamer who has longed—and who has not? —to make the world a better place. It touches some primordial yearning for perfection in us, for the impossible whole, the unattainable goal, and we renounce it with a heavy sigh of sadness to return to the wicked world, and soldier on as best we can.

But supposing you were not so easily cast down? Supposing you burned with the fire of faith that a nobler life was possible for you and all those about you, and supposing this fire grew to an incandescent ecstasy that would not be denied? And supposing you were already enthroned as a living god, king of the greatest empire the world had ever known, that your word was absolute law, your lightest wish a command? Would it not then be possible to realize the dream, to shatter the old world to bits and create the heart's desire?

There was a man who thought it would. "King of the South and North, who liveth in Truth, son of the Sun, living in Truth, lord of the diadems, Akhnaton, great in his duration."

This mysterious mystic, whose origins are obscure, known as the first monotheist, as the heretic Pharaoh, or (by his enemies) as "that criminal," did indeed suddenly, violently thrust a new religion into life. A religion so strange, so pure, so full of love and beauty that for a moment it took the world's breath away.

"There shall be no more worship of stone giants to strike fear into the hearts of men, no more pandering to death and the secret police of the underworld, no more power and extortion by a greedy priesthood. The god Amon is evil. His name shall be obliterated from the face of the earth, hammered from the gold, chiseled from the stone."

In some such manner must decrees have gone forth. Akhnaton abandoned his capital, Thebes, to move a few miles down the river to found his new life. All was done in haste, for there never could be time for all he aimed to do. So there arose along the banks of the Nile this pathetic little brick city (for the local stone turned out to be too friable to use), with its great palace, its beautiful temple, its open-air altars where the new Lord of the Universe, Aton, the Sun, was worshipped at sunrise and sunset with offerings of fruit and flowers.

> When thou sendest forth thy rays
> All the trees and plants flourish,
> The birds flutter
> Their wings uplifted in adoration of thee.
> Thou art he who created the man-child in woman
> Who makest the seed in man
> Oh thou God whose powers no other possesseth.

The few pictures that remain of that idyllic period are full of gaiety, happiness, innocence and love. The sculptors and craftsmen, inspired by the ecstasy of the Pharaoh, used their new freedom to create works of art of unsurpassed beauty. The rays of the life-giving Sun are portrayed streaming down on him. With his swollen belly and scraggy neck, the bas-reliefs show him not as a formal statuesque dummy—as Pharaohs had always been shown before—but as a man "living in truth," with his wife, Nefertiti, and his children around him.

But strange complications begin to cloud the story. The Pharaoh's mother, Queen Tiy, seems to supplant his wife. A power struggle develops. The pacifist mystic ignores all matters of state, and when the insurgent kings at the frontiers of empire begin to rebel, Egyptian guards are forbidden to fight. Insurrection and treason go unchecked.

Anguished cries for help from marooned governors remain unanswered. Vassals no longer pay tribute. The Empire begins to crumble. A crisis is at hand.

Suddenly, as mysteriously as it had begun, the dream ended. Nobody knows how Akhnaton died. Nobody knows what befell the dazzling Nefertiti. No tombs, no monuments have been found. Akhnaton's name and titles were ruthlessly destroyed by a vengeful priesthood, expunged from the face of the earth. So, for 3,000 years even an outline of the extraordinary fate of this tragic, lonely man was lost—a Pharaoh doomed to die tens of thousands of years before his time, for daring to try to establish a kingdom of peace and love.*

But still his poems of piety and innocence ring down the ages:

The chick in the egg that peepeth in the shell
Thou givest breath to him within it to maintain him.
Thou hast prepared for him his time, to break his way
     from the egg,
And he cometh forth from the egg to peep at his time,
And so he walketh upon his feet . . .

•

Now we began to leave the Nile on our left, cutting straight across the desert. At one point it swelled out and

Oedipus and Akhnaton, a most remarkable book by Immanuel Velikovsky, pieces together hitherto unsuspected threads in the story of the heretic Pharaoh, and suggests strange links in the legend to masterpieces in Greek drama written a thousand years after the protagonists had vanished from the scene.

then was cut abruptly. This was the Aswan Dam. When we brought it abeam, we knew we should have covered half the distance.

This stretch of desert is the only one which lives in my memory. It seemed so vast, so unbearably lonely. From horizon to horizon the sand rose and fell like the rollers of some endless sea. Here and there were patches where the winds had blown the sand clear off the rock beneath, leaving huge livid bruises, clotted scars of dried blood. Yet I began to feel how men could come to love the emptiness, the enormous vistas, the struggle just to keep alive, the challenge, the mystery of it all. I remembered the great explorer, Doughty, robbed of his camel, setting out into the desert alone with nothing but his saddlebags. "Happy is the man (he said) who carries all his worldly possessions on his head." Here everything was fined down to the dry sinews of survival. Nothing mattered but water. Water was life. And when men of desert blood came to abundance of it, as they had in southern Spain, how they gloried in it! The palaces in Granada were poems to water, they lived around pools of water, water flowed through their courtyards, the floors of the rooms were runneled with water, fountains praised Allah, the very balustrades of the staircases ran to the music of water.

The dome of blue was paling out, the sun was lower than I liked, the Nile was sliding backwards again. Where we joined it should be Wadi Halfa, but I could not see it. We should only just make it before dark. We were doing a bit too much. Only a few days ago we had left Milan. 800 miles a day. We'd been lucky at Athens, hardly made it to Cairo, and now here again we should only just scrape in. Tomorrow we would cut it down to one hop only. Khartoum would be quite enough.

So my thoughts went as my eyes scanned the desert ahead. Long shadows from the dunes mottled the hollows with blue. Night was coming up, but there ahead was something. A cluster of huts on the river, a white building, beyond, points of light on the ground, flames flickering. It must be a flare path—an old paraffin flare path—shades of the First World War! Somebody was taking no chances, giving us all the help he could to get us down safely. Even if it was not yet quite dark, he would be on the safe side.

We rolled in and were flagged to a place on the tarmac by an enormous Sudanese grinning from ear to ear. Welcome was written all over that happy black face. What a relief to be in the Sudan!

"Good evening, sah! Very glad to see you, sah! 'Nother fellah comin' 'long behind you, sah."

"The Anson?"

"Yessah. See the lights, sah."

He pointed and we picked out the Anson far above. We heard the engines cut and watched the falling curve of lights. Now it was quite dark, and asking our Sudanese friend—for so we immediately thought of him—to have us filled up for an early start, we watched the Anson put down, and all piled into a bus to drive down to the Wadi Halfa Hotel.

8

To Khartoum

THE HOTEL AT WADI HALFA was a gracious relic of the "good old days." Pretty chintzes covered sofas and arm-chairs, so amply padded that with the temperature around 100° Fahrenheit it was impossible to sit in them. The water was boiling in the bath taps, when all we longed for was an iced shower. The terrace provided a romantic view of disconsolate pelicans delousing themselves on the sand-banks of the Nile, and the food could not have been bettered in Bournemouth. But the bed linen was fresh, the room spotless, and the cost extremely reasonable. I should add, perhaps, that it was a government-run place and set a standard no private Sudanese concerns could approach. It suited the Anson crew so well that they overslept, and we were well on our way to Khartoum the next morning before they were stirring.

It was a long stint, almost 500 miles. Another 500 miles of that desert, which was beginning to seem endless with nothing but the everlasting Nile for company. But at least we couldn't very well miss our way, and provided the engines kept running we were bound to arrive. By now the little cockpit was as cosy and familiar as home. The gauges showed our tanks were full. Oil pressure stood steadily at 50 p.s.i. The throttles set for cruising, well within their maximum, told us the engines were turning over 1,500 times a minute. The air-speed indicator read 110 m.p.h., the altimeter showed 12,000 feet, and below us was the world!

The Nile south of Wadi Halfa takes a mild bulge to the west, so holding our southerly course, we left it on our right, but took good care to keep it just within gliding distance in case of emergencies. Nobody looking down on that terrible emptiness stretching to the four horizons could fail to take such an obvious precaution. But what a bore it was! On earth a man could relate to a tree, to a house, to a hill, but how could he relate to 8,000 square miles of nothing?

From the earth, the height, the isolation, the detachment of a pilot was godlike. He could not distinguish the shape of a man. A visitor from Mars might come that close and never know the species existed. It was quite possible to accept the old idea that heaven was in the skies and that the gods occasionally glanced down on the earth.

From a great height, all human problems seem petty and unimportant, so from time immemorial man has thought it advisable to call God's attention to the human predicament. Tradition had it there were various efficacious ways of doing this. You could, like the Buddhists, set off fireworks, whose bangs he would be sure to hear. You could offer him a good square meal in the shape of a bullock or a ram—or even your favorite daughter. You could fast, you could pray, but gradually the glimmer of an idea arose that perhaps what you wanted was not what you needed. God saw things differently. Thy will be done . . .

This detachment, in a very simple practical way, was obvious to any pilot. But he was only in the position of being a temporary god. Although he might have had opportunity to see all this, he was just as earthbound as the next man. But was it possible that man was, as has been said, "the pupil of God's eye?" Was it possible that having no body, no functions himself, He needed us, saw through us, felt through us, suffered and died through us? And that He had compassion and pity for us because we were His functions, an integral part of Him? Was this the sense and meaning of man's life? Maybe. But these were questions no one could answer.

Meanwhile, the heat was intense. Olga had stripped to the waist. Glancing down every now and then at her perfect torso, I was soon deep in quite another train of thought which evidently could not be consummated as we had no automatic pilot. She had long ago given up looking at "the view," and to pass the time was busy with her needle, creating a pair of panties which I hoped she would model for me later. It was a strange setting for domestic bliss. All we needed was a cat and a log fire.

We were alone, quite alone. What could be more private than 12,000 feet over the Sahara? I leaned over to touch her breasts. She smiled and looked up, lazily lifting her parted lips to mine. Then, suddenly, I caught sight of something beyond the window. The wing tip of the Anson was swaying there, not twenty yards away, and all the crew were at the windows with their cameras pointed!

"Gosh! Cover yourself, love, we've got company."

Olga covered herself pretty smartly.

"The snoopers!" I was looking at them laughing at us. "Creeping up on us like that."

"Well, darling, it's the R.A.F. tradition. You ought to have kept a better lookout."

I knew the Anson had the legs on us but they must have stepped on it to catch up to us. Now they throttled down and we continued in formation.

As a matter of fact, when I got over the intrusion I was glad they'd turned up. Ahead, I'd seen a collection of mud huts on the river bank. The Nile had curled back across our course. We were over Merowe. Here the river began its enormous swing northeastwards in a huge loop above the fifth cataract. This loop was more than 250 miles across, and the river did not return to its north–south bearing until we reached Khartoum. To cut the loop, a single-track railway had been built. This saved goods and travelers several days on the river. Now we were coming up to the loneliest stretch of the Sudan, the Bayuda Desert, where we were not supposed to fly without escort. Although nobody had bothered us about this, to have the Anson with us gave us a comfortable feeling. Below we could just see the hairline of the railway, and the little box huts that marked the stations, numbered one to six. It was the only sign of man in that vast waste. So, for the next two hours, we flew in company.

There is something very satisfying and exciting about formation-flying. We admire the beautiful maneuvers of the aerobatic teams, demanding the highest pilot skills, without really understanding what is involved. When flying together—and particularly close together—you cannot just set your throttle at the speed of the leader and leave it at that. Constant adjustments are necessary, and it is on the delicacy and accuracy of these adjustments that perfect formation-flying depends. This is no problem for the leader. He simply sets a course and speed well within the compass of the rest. His business is to lead the formation. The others are obliged to trust him blindly, for they have no time to look around. Their whole attention is concentrated on "keeping station." This concentration is very exacting and, after a time, exhausting. Swans, geese, ducks and other birds who fly in formation frequently change their leaders. This is not because one thinks he knows the way better than his companions. It is because the leader's position is one of "rest," and each takes the least arduous position in turn.

In an open formation, with perhaps 100 yards or more between the aircraft, the strain is not so great. But in tight formations it's a different matter. In 1918 we used to fly Camels in formations so close that our wing tips actually overlapped. There was just about ten feet between us, and you had to trust the skills of the team pretty well before you dared come that close. The smallest mistake could be fatal. It is not just a matter of fine adjustment in speed—although the pilot's hand never leaves the throttle: there are continuous small movements on all three controls to keep an exact relative position in space. Five feet up or down is out of position. Five feet can be wide, or too damned close. And all this when traveling at high speed demands an extremely sensitive and delicate touch. The effect from one aircraft to another is a slow, lazy, swaying up and down, in and out, like bubbles in oil. It is exhilarating. The pilots can see the whites of each other's eyes, and when in the early days we knew we had got our formation pretty well perfect, we would give each other the high sign. We knew the risks and we were proud of our skill.

But on that far-away morning back in October 1947, approaching Khartoum, things were less complicated. I was in the fortunate position of being the leader. The old Anson swayed near my starboard wing tip, not close enough to be alarming, but close enough to give that warm feeling of companionship in the air. We tried to speak to each other on the R.T., in fact I could see the captain mouthing into his microphone, but as usual there was no dice, and we soon gave up.

At last the Nile came snaking back from its huge detour, as we reached the last railway station. There was the little town where they met. Soon, Omdurman and Khartoum loomed up through the ground haze, a straggling mass of mud huts, brown as the desert, sprawled along one side of the river. On the other side we could make out the palms in the streets of Khartoum, the green of public gardens, and a few big buildings.

The Anson captain waved, and opening his throttles, pulled ahead, diving into the murk. We followed, sorry to be leaving the cool upper air. Soon we were down to 8,000 feet and started being thrown about by the "bumps," the up-currents of boiling air, rising turbulent from the scorching desert. When we touched down and I swung up the window of the Gemini, I remember I actually flinched. It was like opening the door of an oven.

9

To Juba

THERE MAY BE HOTTER PLACES in the world than Khartoum. If so, I certainly don't want to visit them. The drab, parched, dusty place seemed like the world's end—as it had been to General Gordon, all those years ago. Reading about that strange Victorian hero, with his brandy and his Bible, I had never before taken the heat into account. The long-drawn-out siege of the town by hordes of fanatical tribesmen led by the "mad Mahdi," the stoic (and quite unnecessary) defense of the wretched place until food and ammunition were exhausted, the general's "classic" death, in full dress uniform at the head of a flight of steps, defiant to the end—all this had taken place in temperatures that quite demoralized us before we reached our hotel on the banks of the Nile. How on earth had he stuck it? The sweat poured off us, running down our arms, trickling down our noses. Talk about dehydration! We were being dried up so fast that even the pint-size glasses at the hotel—the largest glasses I've ever seen in my life—could not put back what we were losing. These were the Turkish-bath conditions in which Gordon had withstood the rigors of a medieval siege.

And none of it need have happened! That was the irony of the situation. Gordon had been sent out under the strictest instructions not to smash the Mahdi, but simply to withdraw a small Egyptian garrison, and any Christians who wanted to leave, northwards to the comparative safety of Egypt.

But no sooner had he arrived in Khartoum than, with a blatant disobedience of orders, he ignored all ideas of evacuation and prepared the town for siege. He sent letters to the Mahdi, instructing him to cease hostilities. This fanatical religious leader, with 20,000 very aggressive tribesmen under his command, replied by inviting Gordon to embrace "the true faith," otherwise he would cut off his head. Gordon scoffed, but saw that he might need help. Not much, "Two hundred men would do it."

Today, with radio airlifts and parachute drops, such a situation could never have arisen. But Gordon's sole communication with the outside world was a single telegraph line, over which his signals, tapped out in Morse, were

relayed through Cairo to London. When a couple of tribesmen cut the wire, there was silence from the Sudan.

But when at last the gravity of the situation really got
through (mainly through the *Times* correspondent who
was still in Khartoum), England began to grow alarmed.
Strangely, nobody censured Gordon for flagrant disobedience of orders. His lonely stand against odds had made
him a national hero, a warrior saint, and now the country
was going to lose him, Khartoum, and the national honor
as well. There was an outcry. Queen Victoria herself took
an indignant hand in it. Messages were sent, exhorting
him to hold out. Help was coming. But the messages never
arrived, nor did the help. Khartoum fell.

It was not until fourteen years later, at the Battle of
Omdurman, that the sway of the Union Jack was at last
restored. It took 22,000 seasoned troops, with the latest
weapons, to defeat 44,000 tribesmen who, with fanatical
bravery, charged machine guns and artillery again and
again, to leave 27,000 dead on the field. The Mahdi had
been overcome, vengeance had been taken.

Things had changed a good deal since those days. The
British residents we met never mentioned Gordon. They
were a washed-out lot, drained of all energy by the heat,
and made us laugh by saying that it was "cool in the evenings." Anything under 100° Fahrenheit was cool. But at
least we had an electric punkah. It was installed below the
high ceiling of our quarters, and turned slowly but effec-
tively, creating a night-long breeze that was a lifesaver.
Alternately taking showers and lying wet and naked on

our beds to cool off by evaporation, we passed a sleepless night, and it was a great relief to take off the next morning and climb through the blanket of heat to the cooler air above. Khartoum, as far as we were concerned, was a wonderful place—to get away from.

•

In the middle of the town the Nile divides. The two rivers run parallel, about 100 miles apart, and after keeping this up for 200 miles, the left-hand river (if you are flying south), the Blue Nile, wanders off east to Abyssinia, while the White Nile, which we were following, continues southwards to rise in Uganda. But Uganda lay another 1,000 miles towards the equator, and between us and it lay, so we had been warned, the most remote and dangerous passage in our flight. Our immediate destination that morning was Malakal, a small town on the banks of the Nile, which lay about 500 miles south of Khartoum. It marked the southern limit of the desert. After that we should be finished with the featureless emptiness from which it sometimes seemed we never could escape. We should also be finished with the Nile as an aid to navigation. For 1,000 miles it had been the only feature in the landscape. After Malakal, we were told, it wouldn't be easy to follow. Back in town, seeing the blue thread on the map, we could not quite understand why.

Khartoum was 1,276 feet above sea level. Although we were now little more than 10° north of the equator, we hoped the higher ground might make the climate less

oppressive. But also, it would make our takeoff more sluggish, because the air would be thinner 2, 3, or 4,000 feet
up. However, this was no immediate problem, and we
looked forward to the end of the desert with rising spirits.
The equatorial jungles ahead might be no less dangerous
than the desert, but they promised at least to be more
interesting.

The human memory is a marvelous thing, and I am
certain that every act, every scene, every face, every
thought is faithfully recorded by it. But finding those re-
cordings is a different matter. Some spring up clear and
fresh, as if they happened yesterday. Others are far more
deeply hidden. In fact, 99 percent of our impressions are
lost and cannot be recalled. Our search into memory is
triggered off by another part of the brain, a sort of control
room, which initiates the inquiry, which says, for instance,
Khartoum—Malakal, Khartoum—Malakal, what do I remember about that? The impulse of recall sets off through
the labyrinthine storerooms of the past, but somewhere
along the way there is a blockage. It gets lost among the
catacombs, and cannot reach its destination. There is silence. No bells ring. A nil return. I remember almost nothing.

All I can fish up from my cellars about that morning is
blurred, vague. The sand seemed deeper in tone, the river
banks higher. Far ahead there are black dots in the sand.
There seemed to be more of them on the horizon. What
can they be? They must be trees—trees! This seems a sort
of miracle, and as we approach them we discern their

color, very dark, almost black. Now they are growing thicker, and before we reach Malakal, the earth seems almost normal. It is an enormous relief. It rests our eyes. We are jubilant, we laugh with pleasure. The airfield seems to stand above the river on higher ground, the town below it. The men who receive us wear a deep red fez, ornamented with a golden crescent and star . . . But all this is misty, obscure, disjointed. It may be incorrect, for sometimes, if memory fails us and will not give an answer, we make up a false one to deceive ourselves and others. The only thing I am quite sure about is that we did reach Malakal, and were later there joined by the Anson, whose crew had promised to escort us along the next hop to Juba.

But if the morning's memory is vague, the afternoon's is vivid. As we rose from Malakal, the contrast seemed extraordinary. We had been over the desert so long we could not believe we were suddenly over jungle. Green stretched out ahead of us, and there were actually clouds —clouds! When had we last seen clouds? Approaching the coast of Africa over the Med—it seemed a year ago. And the Nile, doggedly fighting its way through the desert wastes? The Nile had disappeared, literally disappeared under hundreds of square miles of rushes and water plants. It had turned into a hundred Niles. So clearly, as we had been warned, we would have to abandon it as an aid to navigation. What could we substitute? Nothing but the compass. The compass would have to lead us to Juba, another few hundred miles to the south.

This land below us that afternoon was known as the

Sudd, a chartless jungle, practically uninhabited, a formi-
dable barrier to those adventurous souls who set out to
drive a motor car from Cairo to the Cape. It was only
possible to get through at all during the short dry season,
and then only by a track which was washed away every
year. But that afternoon it looked to us the most gentle-
manly sort of jungle we had ever seen. Everything was
restful, welcoming and peaceful. The overall impression
was that of parkland: clumps of trees, stretches of green
grass: we almost expected the Hunt to emerge from behind the clumps. But it was a gross deception, for the
parkland was elephant grass, twelve feet high, with
swamp at its roots, and the trees had their feet in water.
It was no place to be forced down. In fact, one unfortunate
pilot, doing the trip gallantly—but perhaps foolishly—in
an old De Havilland Moth, had engine failure somewhere
here and it took ten days to find him and get him out.

It was hard to believe, for scenically, from 12,000 feet, it
was the most beautiful stretch of landscape we covered in
Africa. Perhaps this was chiefly due to the strange cloud
formations over which we flew. There were many bush
fires below us in the jungle. Had these sprung up spon-
taneously, or been lit by tribes living there? We never
knew. But they raised blue columns of smoke which stood
vertically in the still, tropical air. Each column was topped
by a white cap of cloud, and the sun's rays, striking down,
lit the smoke shafts obliquely, so the whole sky seemed to
be trailing veils of translucent blue. As the cloud caps were
well below us at about 8,000 feet, we sailed clear over this

magical pattern of white and blue and green, and it seemed at the time a sort of gift, a repayment for all those miles of desert where our eyes had ached from the glaring emptiness of sky and earth.

The Anson, which had taken off well after us, now came up alongside and we continued south together, toward a point in the jungle we had agreed beforehand to investigate. This was Bor, and it was near here, we had been told, that the largest elephant herd in the world was said to wander. As we had never seen elephants in the wild, the prospect excited us. By now we had left the "parkland" jungle. A solid floor of green lay beneath us, and how were we going to find elephants in that? There was only one way. We should have to go down to ground level and quarter the area. The Anson shut off and began to sink towards the treetops. But we did not follow. Frankly, I funked it.

There is no experience in flying so exciting as "contour chasing," as we used to call it in the early days. Skimming over the ground about fifty feet up, zooming up the hillsides, careering down the valleys, you get quite a special view of the countryside. The speed of an aircraft disappears once you are well clear of the ground, and modern airliners flying at perhaps 400 or 500 m.p.h. seem to be almost motionless to the passengers that fly in them. But at fifty feet, even 100 m.p.h. seems terrific, and there is no thrill for a pilot equal to banking on his wing tip between a couple of elms, or just missing the weathercock on the top of a church steeple. It demands more and more skill the closer you cut it, and it is so exhilarating to see the world flying past that many a man has become drunk with the marvelous sense of skill and freedom that it gives. Dozens of good men have killed themselves taking these intoxicating risks. But I had learnt my lesson after being sent to identify the charred remains of two of my own boys, who had cut it too fine and just touched a power line with their wing tip. With a flash the aircraft had catapulted into the ground and caught fire. There was nothing left when that sheet was raised from the marble slab but cinders.

By now the Anson was shooting about above the jungle in all directions. He was evidently having a lot of fun, but when he did not circle over one particular spot, I concluded he had failed to find the herd. We remained sedately above, for I saw no point in taking risks of that kind for the sake of a fleeting glimpse of what I had often contemplated, complete with trumpeting and buns, in the wilds of Regent's Park. But then I was pushing fifty, and the Anson captain was twenty-five. It makes a lot of difference. Soon, after kicking up his aerial heels, the Anson rejoined us and we soldiered on.

Flying a compass course is, as I have said, a sort of act of practical faith. You must get to heaven, but in the meantime you aren't quite sure whether you will. Usually at the end of your trip you expect to find some obvious landmarks—a coast, a river, a town—but this time, all we could expect to find was a clearing in the jungle big enough to hold a runway. And this was, after all, a very small island in a very big sea. So it was a relief to spot an arrangement of small gray huts, an open space, then a runway and a windsock. This was Juba. We touched down happily, having covered a thousand miles since breakfast.

During the Second World War, I had served under Whitney Straight in the Mediterranean, when he was running Transport Command, his group stretching from Casablanca to Bahrain. Now he had taken on the management of B.O.A.C., and with typical thoughtfulness and generosity, when he heard I was making this trip, he sent a signal down the line that station commanders were to treat us like V.I.P.s. It saved a lot of bothersome details with customs, landing fees, refueling and the like.

Juba is a pretty isolated spot, but Simpson, as I think he was called, the staging post commander, evidently following these instructions, put himself out to be helpful and hospitable to us. He suggested putting us up for the night in his bungalow, and we gladly accepted. But as we stepped into his living room, we were stopped dead in our tracks and scared out of our wits to see, lying curled up on the sofa, a fully-grown black panther.

"Get out of there, Rajah!" Simpson shouted, as he followed us in. The panther stretched, blinked lazily at his master with those huge yellow eyes, slid off the couch and curled up on the floor.

"Pay no attention to him," said Simpson, seeing our consternation. "Quite harmless. Had him since he was a cub."

All the same, I confess that though we carried it off as

best we could, I found myself keeping a very wary eye on the brute as he followed Simpson about from place to place, with that slow loping walk, and was glad when we had settled down with our drinks and Rajah came to sit with his master. Simpson pulled his ears, patted his head, scratched his neck, until Rajah was purring like a tractor.

"He's a fine chap, isn't he?" said his owner proudly. "I'm on my own here, and he's good company. Somebody to come back to. And hunt! You should see him with snakes. No chance of finding a rattler in your boots with him around."

We talked with our host of this and that, told him about our trip, gave him news of the U.K. and so on, but every time he got up to get cigarettes, or refill our glasses, Rajah followed him like a shadow, rubbing against him and purring. I couldn't get over it.

"Is he safe?" I asked. "I mean, how do you manage with callers, servants and so on?"

"No trouble with white people, but of course no native dare come near the place. He smells them a mile off. He tolerates my own servants, but they do treat him with a certain amount of respect."

"I should think so!" I laughed.

"It's really a question of not being afraid," Simpson went on. "I'm quite sure wild animals, especially the big cats, can smell fear. But if they know you're not afraid of them it's perfectly all right." He laughed abruptly. "For instance, only the other day a funny thing happened. I was walking across the airfield for lunch when I saw Rajah sitting out on the runway. I don't like him being out there, so I shouted at him to get on out of it. He looked at me but didn't move, so I walked up to him and cuffed him soundly round the ears. He growled a bit the way he does when he doesn't want to be moved, and then loped off into the jungle. Then I saw his flank had a scar on it. It wasn't my Rajah! When I got back, here was my old brute lying on the sofa!"

"Good God!" I ejaculated, "you were lucky to get away with that."

Simpson laughed. "Probably one of his girlfriends coming on heat. I don't see him for a week when that happens. But it's all a question of fear. If they know you're not scared of them and won't harm them, they won't attack you."

Maybe, but I was glad that Rajah didn't decide to come and curl up on our bed for the night.

10

To Nairobi

THE PROSPECT BEFORE US the next morning was exhilarating. Not only did we expect to reach the equator—the invisible halfway house of Africa—but we should actually get back into country which was at least partially "civilized." There would be roads—even a railway. This seemed very important to us. Flying a compass course is all very well, but it's a relief to be able to check it against real live landmarks.

At first that morning, leaving Juba, it was much the same. Below on our right were the miles of tall rushes and trees which marked the course of the White Nile. But the wide expanse of river bed seemed a bit narrower, and ahead we saw—for the first time in days—the outline of hills, enormously welcome after the monotonous horizon of the desert to the north. Earth began to show red in the clearings between huge stretches of jungle. There were signs of native settlements, a few thatched huts edged with trees. People—there were actually people living there far below us. It seemed exciting and surprising, so much had we come to think that the entire continent was uninhabited. People, however strange, however remote, gave us a new bond with the earth, and we pointed out to each other tracks in the clearings, canoes at the river's edge. It all seemed marvelous. Then there was actually a broader track, a dirt road. A real road, and far over on the right a hard clean line—a railway! It was terrific. That must be the line that ran south to Entebbe. We were in Uganda.

To pass the time we began trying to pick out the various features along the line. Lakes, settlements, and then small towns. We noted signs of cultivation: sheds, farms, ploughed fields of deep red earth. I suppose it was in fact all very simple and primitive, but the feeling of elation persisted. The desert we had crossed was terrible country after all. We'd come through safely, but underneath there'd always been the anxiety, which although neither of us had ever mentioned it, had forbidden any carefree feelings. We had both always been on guard. For almost 2,000 miles a forced landing would at best have been very awkward, but now it didn't matter. If by bad luck we had to put down, we could be sure of help. We should probably even find people who spoke English! It was an enormous relief.

To our enthusiastic eyes it all looked like splendid country. Among these hills lay not only the source of the Nile, but at least two big tributaries of the Congo, which rolled away westward to the distant Atlantic. There were lakes, too: Lake Albert, the head of the Nile, Lake Kyoga, and far ahead, what looked like a sea; the northern shore of Lake Victoria Nyanza. On its shore we should find Entebbe, Uganda's capital, and land there, bang on the equator.

At the time I don't remember that I bothered to calculate how far we had come, where we were in respect to the overall length of the trip. It's only now, studying the map of Africa, that in the cautious way of old age I shake my head at the risks we took, at the distances we covered in that tiny airplane. We must have been mad, I say to myself, quite mad. But at the time I never thought of risks or danger. I trusted my luck and my skill. It is, I believe, the right way to live. The maps, now I come to think of it, were a sort of joke in themselves. There was pretty well nothing on them. They covered each section of our route at a scale of about twenty miles to the inch. Back in the U.K., I had carefully cut them into strips in which our track (with the magnetic course written against it) lay down the center, and showed a belt of about a hundred miles on either side. Each map was carefully numbered, to be used in turn. But large sections of Africa were then hardly mapped at all, so there was very little information on those maps—and some of it incorrect anyway. Besides, there were huge tracts of country in which there weren't any landmarks.

Nobody, until they fly over it as we did, can grasp the scale of Africa. A modern jet, traveling at about 500 m.p.h., shrinks the enormous distances to a few hours, and this, coupled with the great height at which it flies, leaves the passenger with no sense of scale. From his comfortable seat he gets an oblique view of a distant, misty, almost featureless world. He has no connection with it, it doesn't concern him. He has no responsibility for the aircraft's safety, and its arrival at some destination is taken for granted. At any moment, radio beacons and beams tell the captain exactly where he is, not in respect to the earth, but in relation to the goal toward which he is bound. In addition, he has ample reserves of power and fuel, and all his navigational aids are duplicated. At any moment, he can speak to the ground and be sure of help in any doubt or emergency. It's a very real morale booster. His anxieties (which are by no means to be shrugged off) are basically confined to the times when he is circling "stacked up" over crowded air terminals in dirty weather, and the actual touch-down when the ceiling is zero and there is fog or snow on the runway. But he has no *constant* anxiety.

I do not in any way want to pretend that there was anything heroic about our flight to Africa. It was only a rather long "cross-country." But the fact remains that when you have little reserve of power, and cannot maintain height on one engine if the other should cut, when you have no automatic pilot to take the strain out of the actual flying of the airplane for hours on end, when you cannot communicate with the ground in emergency, and have no navigational aids beyond a map and a compass, then all the problems facing you are different from those confronting an airline pilot. Everything takes place against an ever-present background of anxiety, and you develop a hypersensitive ear to the running note of the engines.

Our friends in the Anson had taken off from Juba after us. They were pressing straight on to Salisbury. They had escorted us through dicey stretches of desert and jungle, and we were sorry to see them go. By now they must be miles ahead of us. Just for a joke, I thought I would call them up on our little radio telephone. It wouldn't work of course, but there was no harm in trying. When their answer came back loud and clear, I was astonished. We pinpointed our position. They must have been a hundred miles away, and our set had a range of only twenty-five miles! It was fantastic—the only time the set had worked on the whole trip! The clichés of goodbye seemed to have some meaning as we said them from our cockpits, so far apart, high in the lonely sky.

"Have a good trip. Over."

"Same to you and Mrs. Lewis. Happy landings. Over and out."

We put down at Entebbe.

•

Ever since leaving Cairo, we'd been flying due south. For 2,000 miles the bearing had hardly changed. Now we were bound for Nairobi, and that meant turning almost due east, along the northern shores of Lake Victoria. The size of this lake alone gives some idea of the scale of Africa. It's practically square, over 200 miles across and almost 300 miles north to south. A vast inland sea of 60,000 square miles—yet it shows as no more than an ink blot on the map of the whole continent!

Standing on the tarmac overlooking the lake, I'd noticed, far away along the shore, a curling plume of black smoke rising several hundred feet into the air. I could see no signs of a chimney, yet it didn't look like a fire, drifting slowly out over the water. Were there, I inquired, the beginnings of light industry starting up over there? The medical officer to whom I spoke laughed indulgently.

"Looks like smoke, doesn't it? Actually, it's flies."

"Flies?"

"A sort of plague of flies. Don't get it every year. Quite harmless, but it makes the shore along that way a bit unpleasant. Wouldn't advise you to investigate, or fly through it or anything. Make an awful mess of your airplane."

When we took off from Entebbe we flew east along the

northern shores of the lake. We kept a sharp lookout for this unusual hazard, but the plague of flies must have drifted or settled, for we saw nothing. The picturesque coastline, with its indented bays and many islands, would probably have seemed more interesting to us than it did had we not seen a heavy blanket of cloud sitting firmly on the tops of the mountain range ahead. Somehow we had to get through that if we were to reach Nairobi.

All this part of the world is one vast plateau, whose "baseline" lies around 4,000 feet. Our map told us that the peaks ahead rose to 7,000, 8,000 and even 10,000 feet. This meant, as I've explained previously, that with our limited ceiling, even when we were as high as we could get, there wouldn't be much to spare—even on a clear day. When the peaks were covered we daren't take risks. We should have to winkle our way through the valleys between them.

After two hours over the water we at last came to the end of it at a little lakeside town called Kisumu. Here, our map told us, was the terminus of a railway, called the Mau escarpment, which snaked its way through the mountains ahead, and would, if we could manage to follow it, lead us out into the Rift Valley and so on to Nairobi. But with the cloud cutting off the mountain tops we should have to sandwich ourselves between them and the very jagged terrain below. It looked as if it might be a bit tricky. Also, as we had been warned about the ferocity of tropical storms, I eyed the heavy clouds, wondering what was in store for us. The country ahead was wild mountain jungle, and although there were a couple of airstrips near our route, the chances of finding them in blinding rain were pretty slim. However, for the moment the rain seemed to be holding off. We began to thread our way through the first deep valleys between the peaks that rose on either side of our precious railway track.

The view ahead—and after all these years I still remember it very clearly—was a white misty V. On either side were the steep black slopes of rock. At the bottom, the line. On top, closing the V, was the flat heavy line of the cloud base. The cloud was evidently thick and took the color out of everything, and made the prospect, all misty grays and blacks, full of foreboding. But now we were committed, and I soon saw something I might have anticipated—the line didn't run straight. It looped and hairpinned through the gorges. But there was one thing I was sure of. If we once lost it, we stood mighty little chance of getting through without hitting something. So, very soon we found ourselves contour chasing like mad. This sort of flying, as I've said, is always pretty dicey, but if you're doing it for fun you can always break off when you like. But now we weren't doing it for fun, we were doing it for survival. Cutting things fine demands quite a lot of pilot skill. Every second the prospect changes. Here is a sudden turn in the line: which way will it go? Mountains ahead, steep turn. Now it's gone into the trees, I've lost it. No, there it is, doubling back on itself. Vertical bank, around we go. Now there's a straight bit. Thank God, actually a train on it—bet the blokes'll be surprised to see us. Here's another narrow bit coming, hold on to the line—there it goes. Well, we can cut that corner. Pick it up at the gorge ahead . . . So it went. I'd forgotten all about engine failure, about risk, about danger: all my faculties and skills were needed to fly the airplane. Of course it was exciting, exhilarating, but it made me sweat. After a solid hour, I was pretty relieved as we emerged from the worst of it to see the prospect open up. The broad flank of a mountain curled away on our left, and on our right was a lake. This was Nakuru. We had made it. We were over the head of the Rift Valley.

Gratefully we turned south into comparatively open country. The railway was still with us, hugging the mountainside on our left, but the valley was broad and we could relax. After skirting another 9,000-foot peak, we came in sight of Lake Naivasha. This is a famous corner of the world, famous for being the place where some of the oldest remains of man have been found. Famous, too, for being the haunt of the world's largest flocks of flamingoes. As Naivasha slid past beneath, we could see along the shores a haze of pale pink—a sort of swathe on the water's edge, where tens of thousands of birds were feeding. Unless you knew, you might have thought the lake was edged with pink sand. Strange, how remote and impersonal everything becomes from the air. Just phenomena to be noted in passing. Things do not touch you in the same way. You are free of them. Who could ever drop a bomb if they felt anything? It takes the mushroom of Hiroshima to move us.

The cloud had lifted a bit, but it was still overcast as we ran on south towards Nairobi. I remember having a sharp feeling of anticipation and excitement. I don't know why Kenya should have this effect, but it does. There is something about it: the green saucers of the extinct craters, the rain forests, the sudden sweep of the plains, the beady unblinking eyes of the lakes; it all emanates a strange challenging beauty. Kenya seems a sort of sorceress, like Circe, impossible to resist. This was an immediate instinctive impression, for that day as we came in to land, I'd never seen it before. But the allure was there. So we put down at Nairobi on the highest airfield of our trip, 5,520 feet above sea level, eager to explore.

11

Kenya

IN 1947, Nairobi was a small, sleepy, easygoing town, famous chiefly as a rendezvous for people going on safari, who could obtain the necessary licenses to kill a specified number of wild animals—lion, elephant, rhinoceros, etc. The whole country was a paradise for game, and already, to preserve it from wholesale slaughter, reserves had been set up as sanctuaries where wild life was protected and no shooting with anything more lethal than a camera was allowed.

This was the first area we had been asked to reconnoiter as a possible place to set up the community to which we were committed. Here, before leaving the U.K., we had arranged to meet Rita. Her husband had served in this area during the war. Both of them knew the country well and had many friends. This, we hoped, would be a big asset in our search, but somehow, although we stayed in Kenya ten days and motored over a lot of country, we never really seriously considered it possible for the sort of life we hoped to lead. The society was too small, too smart, and had a curious whiff of nineteenth-century colonialism about it. Perhaps that was an unjustified feeling, but it was quite enough to put us off.

At the same time, it faced us with a problem. What sort of a place were we looking for? I, for one, had no clear idea. We had always thought of it as a "farm," because in Africa everybody seems to farm. But a farm could be anything from five acres for raising chickens to 10,000 acres to run sheep. It was desirable, we thought, that it should be "fairly large," "fairly cheap," and "fairly isolated," but all that was pretty vague . . .

Life in Africa is very different from life at home. On our crowded island most people are too busy minding their own business to have time for anyone else. They neither know nor care what their neighbors are up to. It is a curious paradox that the more people are crowded together, the more anonymous they become. But here in Kenya there was a very small community, everybody knew everybody else, and everybody else's business. How were we going to fit into that sort of life? We were not in any way "special" people, but we had a special purpose after all, and it was not one we wanted to gossip about at cocktail parties. Isolation was a very relative word. In the U.K. you could be isolated at the far end of a muddy lane. Here people thought nothing of motoring fifty miles for a drink. We didn't want to be thought of as secretive, but rather as if we were harmless, perhaps a little mad. But that role —though it might be true—wasn't going to be an easy one. So after arguing all this back and forth without coming to any clear conclusion, we agreed the only thing to do was to play it by ear. If we came across anything "likely," we could then begin to assess its advantages and disadvantages.

It was quite a celebration when we met Rita in Nairobi, and on schedule. She had flown out and expected to have to wait about for us, if indeed we would arrive at all, which, she confessed, had always seemed a bit doubtful. We had been good friends in the U.K., and from now on she was to join us in our search. We hardly had time to swap news before she swept us off up north to spend a weekend with old friends of hers, at a place called Thompson's Falls. It stood right on the equator, at a height of about 8,000 feet. I found the drive exciting because of the unexpected things that happened. Suddenly to come across a huge bull giraffe at the roadside, staring down at you disdainfully over the *top* of the telephone wires; this was the sort of thing which, for me, only happened in dreams or fairy tales. Then there was the large notice "Beware—elephants crossing," and I felt quite cheated when no herd appeared, slouching across the road with their slow swinging gait. But the most exciting creatures of all were the ostriches.

If I'd been asked to choose a creature which had been created with no thought of camouflage whatever, I would certainly put the ostrich pretty high on the list. Long legs, topped by an awkward bundle of a body at least four feet in the air, and on top of that a long white neck—it was clearly impossible to hide such a beast, and I presumed it had survived because of its terrific legs and its ability to outrun a galloping horse. So when our host, who was driving the car, said, "See! Over there! Ostriches!" I couldn't think what he was talking about. The country on either side of the road was open and arid, miles of dry, yellow, grass-covered rolling hills, and dotted all over them were hundreds of small stunted trees. They had thin trunks, with a black rounded mop on top. They were exactly like ostriches! We stopped the car to look, and for a moment I couldn't see anything but trees. Then one of them moved. Yes, there it was, pecking at something on the ground. An ostrich, perfectly camouflaged in a piece of open grassland with a few bushes!

"And look!" said our host again. "When he raises his neck, the dirty white blends perfectly with the haze in the sky."

Afterwards, whenever we came to that sort of country, we had competitions in ostrich-spotting, but curiously—or perhaps obviously—we never saw ostriches anywhere else. Don't tell me angels haven't been at work here, fitting a big awkward bird that can't fly into a country where it can run freely if pursued, and where it can subsist happily on the grubs and berries of those particular trees. It is the coming together of all the apparently incompatible elements that makes the miracle.

And what a marvelous miracle it is! Eat or be eaten is a law of life, yet nothing wants to be eaten, and it is as if every living thing, from amoeba to elephant, has its own guardian angel who tries with every sort of ingenious device—shape, color, movement, pattern—to protect it from others who would devour it. The battle between the predator and the prey ranges through the whole pyramid of life, and there is not a trick or trap that has not been exploited. Electric shocks, poison darts, imitation camouflage, personal armor, speed, filthy smell—you name it, nature has it. As if the whole creation was an infinitely complex game of chess in which each move was calculated to baffle the enemy. If it was a law of life that you had to eat to live, you had to be pretty smart to be able to do so. And all these tricks and ruses, maintaining a most delicate and subtle balance, preserve the harmony of the whole. Gurdjieff told us that the manifested universe was created to hold time at bay. Left to itself, time would reduce everything to dust. It only fails to do so because of this everlasting re-creation which "winds up," so to speak, everything which would otherwise run down.

On the equator there are no seasons. In the beautiful garden of the house to which we had been invited, everything bloomed at once. It stood in a small dell and had that feeling, common to all the best gardens, of being secret, naturally secluded by the lie of the land around it. Our hosts were keen gardeners, and the place was a riot of blossom. But the strange thing was that none of the flowers were tropical. All the plants and shrubs had come from temperate climates. At 8,000 feet the heat of the equator is mild, so we found ourselves in an English country garden, except that the violets and chrysanthemums, snowdrops and roses, daffodils and Michaelmas daisies all bloomed together. And the problem for the plants must have been when to rest, since there was no cool season to encourage them to do so.

It was, however, cool at night—so cool that we were glad to sleep under blankets in our luxurious bedroom. For the house kept up the high standard of the garden and was just as "English." Old furniture and velvet, oriental rugs on polished floors, bits of Staffordshire in glass-fronted cabinets, and dead sons in silver frames. It might have been lifted straight out of the wealthier reaches of Virginia Water or Beaconsfield—except for the dark servants in their long robes and silk skullcaps, who silently on bare feet seemed always at your elbow, caring for everything and everybody so perfectly it lulled you into a feeling that there was nothing more in life to wish for.

Yet I could not escape the feeling that it was absolutely artificial. It had nothing to do with Kenya. Only one man stood out as different. He turned up at our host's place on Sunday morning. We heard the sound of a motorbike, and Molly, our hostess, smiled, and said with evident pleasure, "That'll be Maurice." He appeared on the terrace, a man

I suppose in his early fifties, rather unkempt, casually, even shabbily dressed, but obviously from his accent and his bearing an educated man, and quite at home in the house. Something in the way our host introduced him, affectionate and yet slightly critical, amused us. "This is my brother-in-law, Maurice. He's practically gone native." Maurice didn't seem in the least put out by this label. He kissed his sister affectionately, shook hands with us, and only then remarked, quite casually, to our host: "You may be glad I've gone native, as you call it, James, in a few months' time. The drums are starting to beat. There's going to be trouble."

"Well, if you keep it out of the garden I'll be much obliged." James, who was a retired general, laughed it off.

Maurice smiled too, and then turned abruptly to me. "Care to have a walk round the garden? There are some plants I want to look at."

I willingly agreed and we moved off, Maurice talking about some new methods of genetic crossing that interested him. "Extraordinary possibilities. Looks as if we shall soon be able to breed roses as big as cauliflowers."

I didn't understand what he was talking about, but we laughed, and as soon as we were out of earshot he apologized, "Excuse my abducting you like this, but I get absolutely browned off with all our crowd. All the residents, I mean—same faces, same chatter day after day, week after week. Anything for a breath of fresh air! Hope you don't mind." Without giving me time to reply he went on, "Tell me, what brings you here? Safari I suppose?"

"Actually"—it was curious how I felt it perfectly natural to talk openly with him although I'd never seen him ten minutes before—"actually, we're looking round for a nice quiet spot to set up a small community."

"Are you, by George? That's interesting; why?"

"Well, we think Europe's done for, and we want to preserve some new ideas. Africa seemed a good choice."

He was thoughtful. "I wonder. I spend quite a lot of time with the tribes round here. Wonderful people. There's a growing feeling . . . They want their country back."

"Then you wouldn't recommend Africa?"

"I think it's going to be tricky for white people—sooner or later. What sort of community are you planning?"

"Well, I suppose basically you could call it a group of people trying to live by some new ideas."

"Religious ideas?"

I hesitated. "Yes, but different."

"How different?"

It put me on a spot. How to explain Gurdjieff's ideas simply and clearly to someone who had never heard of them?

Maurice saw my hesitation and laughed in his charming way.

"I understand your difficulty. You see, I was over in Hollywood a couple of years ago doing some writing. We had a wonderful scenario editor—a Coney Island Jew; whenever we went to him with a half-cooked idea to see if he'd buy it, he used to say, 'Boys, if you can't tell your story in two lines you haven't got a story.' It was absolutely true. I've always remembered it. So tell me, in two lines, what your ideas are."

I hedged. "I don't think you'd understand."

"Try me."

I'm going to make a mess of this, I thought, but after all I can only say what little I've understood.

"Very well. You, I, all of us are asleep, we were born asleep, we live in sleep and we die in sleep."

"You mean we live in a dream?"

"Exactly—in illusion."

"Well, that's not new."

"So we never see the real world. All the chaos, the futility, the stupidity in life comes from the fact that life as we live it is just dreams fighting dreams."

"I suppose that's as good a way of putting it as any."

"So the problem is, how to wake up. How to come out of the dreams—"

"Obviously."

"—and to begin to realize our true human possibilities."

"It's a tall order."

"Yes, but the first thing is to see it, accept that it is so. To get that far is already a big step."

"And then?"

"Then there are disciplines, meditations, to help in this struggle to wake up."

"This can't be for everybody."

"Perhaps not. But it's a challenge to *be,* and that's a challenge that all men should understand and try to meet

—and respect those around them who succeed in being more free. We have no idea what man is capable of. His powers, his possibilities are immense . . ."

"Yes. I believe you. I understand that. You know, when the tribes around here have their big celebrations, they sing and dance and beat their drums night and day, for three days sometimes, till they're in a stupor. It puts them in a very special, detached, exalted state, and then some of them—their witch-doctors, their medicine-men—do seem to acquire powers that make them capable of very strange things. For instance, I'll tell you. The other day I drove home, about fifty miles, after a big tribal do—it lasted three days—I was whacked—walked into my room —it was morning—and there sat their chief medicine-man, helping himself to my tobacco! He greeted me, got up, took my hand, talked a lot about the party and how he'd been glad to see me there enjoying it and so on—all perfectly normal. Then he got up and walked out of the room, and I followed to see him off at the door. When I looked outside, there was nobody there! Nobody at all. He'd vanished. He couldn't possibly have got to my place as quick as I did in the car, so . . ."

"What on earth are you two chattering about?" It was Molly, with Olga. "We thought of going over to the Gibsons' for a drink. Would you care to come?"

"Of course not, Molly." He turned to me. "Sorry to be rude, but those people bore me stiff. Besides, I've got things to do. Well, hope I see you again before you go."

Maurice got up abruptly, shook hands with Olga—"Do excuse me. Those people—well, they've got a very nice place, you'll like it. Enjoy yourselves."

And patting his sister affectionately on the shoulder, he went off.

The Gibsons' house was lovely, and their friends gay and friendly. But Maurice was right. After a month, I could see it, it would be deadly, the same impression that we'd had elsewhere. There were some interesting people, even important people there, but they had no relation with the country or the people in their employ. We wanted to set up a working community. Living for pleasure and letting other people do the work had no place in our philosophy. Kenya was a wonderful part of the world, but it wouldn't do for us. We should have to try further south.

12

To Kasama

WE HOPED Rita would join us to fly the next leg of our trip on to Rhodesia, but she confessed she preferred a more solid-looking airplane than ours, so she would go by scheduled flight and we would meet up in Salisbury. But the day before leaving Nairobi, we accepted an invitation from the game warden to look at his wonderful, small game reserve just outside the town.

It was a wonderful afternoon—the huge, polished mahogany heads of the hippos in the river, the jittery baboons, the scruffy wildebeest, the gazelles, the wart hogs —but the best of the lot were the lions. Our attention was attracted to a spot just off the road where at least twenty cars were standing, parked in a close circle, their hoods pointing inwards. When we came close we saw, surrounded by the cars, three young lionesses just waking up from their afternoon siesta. They stretched, and yawned, and rolled over and licked themselves. Then they got up and sniffed around, perfectly relaxed and at ease as if they had the whole world to themselves. Never once did they look at the cars or the people in them. They simply didn't see them. They didn't exist. Then, one by one, they casually sauntered away through the narrow gaps between the car bodies, still seemingly totally unaware of our presence, and ambled off up the hill.

"Are they off for the evening kill?" I inquired.

"No, not until dusk. Let's go in and have some tea."

It was just before dark when I went out alone with the warden to see if we could find a lion on the hunt. We were lucky. His trained eye saw one long before I could spot the long crouching body edging cautiously up the hill, at the top of which some gnu and gazelles were grazing.

"Let's get ahead of her and watch her come past."

He took the Land Rover off in a wide circle, and we came around to park ahead of the direction in which she was stalking. Then we saw her slowly coming up toward us, a full-grown lioness, in perfect condition. She seemed huge, her long body hugging the ground, the thigh muscles tense under the fur, the paws so stealthily put down as she crept forward. When she was close I could see the nostrils working and the huge eyes glowing in the dusk. She passed within six feet of us and, although we had the engine running, was evidently quite oblivious of our presence, moving slowly, with absolute concentration, on the scent coming down from above.

"Can we see her kill?"

"No. It'll be dark in ten minutes. You don't hear anything. It's quick."

•

Next morning, we were down at the airfield early, going over the aircraft carefully, repacking our luggage, filling up, making a careful check there was no oil drip under the engines. It seems, in retrospect, that I had a constant preoccupation, almost a phobia, about engine failure. I suppose this was partly a hangover from the First World War. In those days the possibility was very real. Even during the Second World War it was part of elementary training for the instructor to cut the engine without warning, and tell the pupil to choose a field and get down into it.

This consciousness of the contours of the earth beneath became so ingrained, so much part of my flying life, that I would find myself automatically registering, "I could get down there," or "No good there." And keeping a very sharp eye on the ground had become second nature to me.

So the habit persisted, as habits do, even when we were "safe" at 10,000 feet, with plenty of time to look around and choose our spot. The trouble was that in this part of the world there didn't seem to be any spots. The earth below looked extremely uninviting. If you did get down all right, where would you be? Perhaps 100 miles from "civilization"—and probably surrounded by hordes of bloody savages, not one of whom spoke the Queen's English! Even if they didn't decide to roast you for dinner, it would be no easy job to find your way out. So although engines were far more reliable, and we had two of them, there was always the nagging feeling that a bit of bad luck might turn up and, in a second, change our carefree security of flight into a nightmare.

All this, I suppose, is an elaborate justification—an excuse—for repeating once again that the terrain that morning, as we took off from Nairobi, was really dreadful. We'd been told that Malakal–Juba was the worst leg, but in my memory this day's leg from Nairobi to Tabora, and on to Kasama—800 miles of trackless country—was far more intimidating.

To start with, the airfield at Nairobi was already 5,000 feet above sea level. This meant that with our ceiling of 12,000 feet, 7,000 feet above the ground was all we could get. The thinner air gave us less lift as we climbed, and the engine, also taking in this thinner air, gave less power. Our take-off run was noticeably longer. The Gemini felt sluggish, reluctant to unstick. She would run and run and run, it seemed she would never get off the ground. But always at the last moment she would lurch into the air, and we breathed again.

The vast flank of Kilimanjaro, all 19,000 feet of it, rose majestically on our left, its peak wrapped in cloud. It was one of the great mountains of the world, whose names are household words. Everest topped the list; Etna, Vesuvius, Olympus were more familiar; Fuji was more romantic (thanks to Hokusai); but even the word Kilimanjaro had a special ring, and like all mountains, it had its own magic, its own gods.

The sight of it was so grand that I found myself actually flying toward it, ignoring for some minutes the compass grid which showed me when I glanced at it that we were wildly off course. Reluctantly we swung around onto our bearing, leaving the magic on our left. If you look at a map of this area you will see that a string of lakes lies almost exactly along the track you need to follow to reach Tabora. Leaving Nairobi the ground drops away quickly to 3,000 feet into a narrow valley, and here you come to the first lake, Magadi, famous for its hot springs. The valley floor then rises rapidly and the next lake, Natron, is up at 5,000 feet. We flew right over the top of this with plenty to spare, for the sky was cloudless and we were up to our usual cruising height. Once past Natron we eased over a bit to our right, for there were mountains ahead. They were glorious—I suppose the finest sights in all Africa. First, Loolmalasin, 12,000 feet, then the whole ridge some 80 miles long, a series of extinct volcanoes, green saucer craters with lakes at their bottoms, and finally Ngorongoro, with its crater over 10 miles across and 2,000 feet deep. This volcanic range rises steeply out of the plain, and we kept it on our left, marveling at what must be one of the strangest mountain formations in the world. Below us lay the Serengeti plain, sliding away to the west for 200 miles before it reached the southern shores of Lake Victoria. All this country figures prominently in any white hunter's book on Kenya, for it is here that the safaris come to camp among the greatest herds of game in the world.

At the southerly tip of the range lay the last of the great lakes, Eyasi, and we checked our position relative to it by a little blue eye of a nameless lake out to our right in the plain. Now the last recognizable landmarks were behind us, and ahead lay a stretch of country which, as I write of it, remains for me the most dreadful of our trip. There were 200 miles of it and no identifiable landmarks whatever. The area was marked on our map as "outside the limits of reliable information," and indeed no map could give any idea of the nature of the country. It was an uncharted waste where thousands of lagoons, sandbanks, river courses were set in endless marshes of swamp and trees. It stretched ahead to the rim of the horizon and teemed, so we had been told before leaving Nairobi, with crocodiles and tsetse flies. You clearly couldn't let your imagination run on the idea of what it would be like to come down in—and get out of—that!

And then, suddenly, the port engine faltered. Bp bp. The rev counter needle was hunting, oil pressure steady, no real loss of power, but in a second I was sweating. Bp bp it went. Nothing to do but hang on. Maybe it would clear. Maybe it was the plugs. Maybe a speck of dust in the petrol. Bp bp bp bp. Then, after what seemed like minutes, but was probably less than fifteen seconds, it cleared. The note was steady. We breathed more easily. But the tension remained.

It seems a fitting moment to record the remarkable composure of my wife throughout the whole trip. After all, it was my trip really. I'd dreamed it up and worked it out. Every day I had the excitement of the next to sustain me. All the time I was flying the airplane. It all depended upon me. And all the time, every day, for almost eight hours, my wife had only to sit there, perfectly passive, often bored, and always hot. In retrospect it would be of course an "experience," something few people do, something she would never forget. But such a perspective isn't one you hold or even think of when you're doing it, and the strain was far greater for her than it was for me. The long sea crossing over the Med, the endless miles of desert, and now the trackless jungle; although we were detached from it all, although as long as we kept going all was well, it could not fail to be anything but an anxious time for her. But if it was so, she gave no sign of it, remaining always in good spirits, buoyant yet quiet, and of course sustaining me by her trust in my ability to get us down safely at the end of the next leg and so to bring the whole adventure to a happy conclusion.

It was a good time for us, perhaps our best time, for differences and incompatibilities were to divide us later.

Harmony gave way to discord, and the end was bitter—as it usually is. But now, in old age, having a built-in propensity to remember the good and forget the bad, I am glad to look back on us there that morning, bound for Tabora, content to be joined in a common aim, a common adventure, a common hope. Had we been able to sustain it, life might have been different. But—and the fault lies chiefly with me—we could not. So wherever she is, and whatever she is doing now, I look back on those few weeks with warmth and gratitude.

When the engine had settled down again we looked at each other, listening to its note.

"Will it be okay?"

It was a question I couldn't answer.

"Hope so. I'll have a look at the plugs when we get down."

I turned back to check the compass course. It would have to lead us to Tabora over those endless swamps. And it did. After two hours, with never a miss from the engine, we sighted the airstrip and put down for a bacon and egg lunch.

Tabora, Kasama. I don't suppose you've ever heard of them. I never should have except for this flight, for they lie off the main commercial air routes, and are nothing but secondary strips with dirt runways, just emergency landing grounds for an airliner in real trouble, and also the site of radio beacons. But because of our limited range they were vital stepping stones for us, enabling us to make our

400-mile hops with enough spare fuel to give us a chance to change our minds and return to our starting point in emergency. Our landing in these remote places was always a bit of an event, for the fields were little used and the boys (and their wives) who were stuck there had almost nothing to do. But they were, nonetheless, essential links in the plans of the Civil Air Authority of Tanganyika which, collaborating with countries north and south, and the airlines overflying this empty country, were setting up (in those days) a network of beams and beacons so that thousands of passengers, who never even knew of their existence, might arrive safely at their destination.

It was the first time we had had the engine cowling off. We took out the plugs and put in a spare set, ran the engine carefully, replaced the cowling and were ready to press on. The midday heat was terrific, the air was dancing over the field, the runway was slightly uphill with trees at one end, there was no wind, and this time I really thought we never should get off. She ran and ran and ran, and at the very last moment came clear, scraping the trees at the end of the airfield, and we slowly gained height after the diciest takeoff of the whole trip.

Our course was now a little more southerly (208° M) and Kasama, our next stop, lay 400 miles away, across another intimidating stretch of country. For the first 200 miles there wasn't a landmark of any kind. Then we ought to pick up the westerly bulge of Lake Rukwa, and seventy-five miles beyond that, the southerly tip of Lake Tanganyika. As this was a good 400 miles long we couldn't very well miss it. Then we should cross the frontier into Northern Rhodesia (which we certainly shouldn't see). After another seventy-five miles we should find Kasama.

Ahead on the horizon, clouds were massing, reminding us that we were now in the southern hemisphere and the seasons were reversed. October was spring down there, and rains could be expected. Back in the U.K. the gen from the Met. Office had warned us about these. The storms usually came up in the afternoon, clouds building up into thunderheads which dispersed again at dusk. Now, today, they lay far to the south, a beautiful range of cumulus bubbling up from the haze, and beckoning me with an almost irresistible fascination. They were such a vivid reminder of the glorious days of my youth during the First World War, when we used to play tag or follow-the-leader among their marvelous peaks and dizzy canyons. Like mountain climbers, we would gain height before them, admiring their solid contours, but keeping well clear until they were below us. Then the game was on. Hand on stick and throttle, we would wheel and dive, plummeting down into the bottomless valleys, zooming on full power up over their peaks, shooting like fish through their caves and tunnels, grey shadowed grottoes beyond which a patch of blue meant a daze of sunlight. In the sheer exhilaration of just being alive, we would pull up into a loop until the whole world was sky, and once over the top, cut the engine and fall headlong to do it all over again. Storming these illusory battlements, more white and luminous than the whitest snow, made us quite drunk with a sort of aerial intoxication that only pilots can know. To pull right up, engine full on, into a vertical stall; then cut the power and fall head-over-heels, with screaming wires, down into a well of white. There was nothing in life to equal this. It was a wild exhilaration and we were drunk with the beauty of the sun and the sky, drunk with speed and mastery of the invisible element that bore us. We lived more freely, more vividly in those few moments than we should ever live again. Indeed the boy with whom I most closely shared this elixir was to die in combat a few weeks later, while I, preserved by some strange talisman, escaped with a slight wound and came safely home. I have often wondered why.

•

Now the worst country was behind us. Our flight was drawing to an end, and its purpose, never far below the surface, began to fill the foreground of our thoughts. Only a couple more hops and we should reach Johannesburg. Then, if we decided to stay in the Union, as seemed likely, our search would enter a more critical stage.

I do not remember that we had the slightest doubt about the outcome of all this. Our trust in the motive that had set us on such a course was absolute. I personally felt no qualms whatever about abandoning England and setting up a new life in Africa. I believed in Bennett. I believed in the teachings of Gurdjieff. As far as I was concerned this was for life—and I can say that today, thirty-seven years later, that trust has never faltered.

But of course at that time it all had quite a different perspective. The efforts we had been taught to make to wake up, to "remember ourselves," not to sleep, did not seem impossible or over-difficult. If we took our work seriously and persisted in our efforts, we should succeed. Heaven seemed just around the corner and a gay and almost carefree attitude enveloped us. Hope would be crowned with success. There would be difficulties of course, but they would be overcome. Whatever the future held, it seemed then, we bore charmed lives because of the sacred impulse that inspired us. In other words, like other pioneers, we were incredibly naïve, optimistic and certain of ourselves. We did not speak much of this. We took it for granted that we should not have embarked on such an aim if we did not believe in it. But it remained a secret impulse, central to life, that inspired our course of action.

Today, after long years of struggle with this work that Gurdjieff described as an effort to "jump over your own knees," I still believe our attitude was right. It sustained us. It was only a sense of failure in the face of an almost impassable barrier that, later, tempered our high hopes with an acceptance of our limitations and our frailty.

Life on earth is as it is—and as God means it to be. Those who wish to hurry its evolution by individual effort do so from personal motives, against the stream, against God. Nobody else is interested. Evolution is not planned on our petty human scale. That such efforts are required of cer-

tain masochistic people is admissible, and that enlighten-
ment is possible is beyond all doubt; but the way is long
and hard. Gurdjieff had warned us: "Blessed is he that hath
a soul and blessed also is he that hath none. But woe to him
that hath it in the making."

•

So we plugged on that afternoon, the crocodiles below
blinking up at us, the tsetse flies buzzing under us, not
remembering at the time to say a prayer or pour a libation
for our safety. But we did it that evening at Kasama, for
it was our wedding anniversary.

13

To Salisbury

NOW THE END of our trip was at last in sight. All the really bad country was behind us, we had crossed from Tanganyika* into Northern Rhodesia, and although the country was not much developed, it was clearly the beginning of civilization. Ahead lay the great copper mines of Ndola, and beyond them Lusaka, the capital and our first stop. It was a short leg, only a bit over 300 miles, and beyond it lay an even shorter hop on to Salisbury.

*Throughout, I have used the old place-names that correspond to the year our flight was made.

The Director of Civil Aviation of Northern Rhodesia, Musprat Williams, had been my commanding officer during the junketing in Greece in 1944. We had signaled ahead to say we might drop in, and had been invited to lunch. So we set off in lively anticipation at seeing someone we knew, and less than three hours later put down in Lusaka without incident.

Lunch developed into quite a party, as such reunions do. Sprat's wife was a beautiful girl and a very good hostess. We had a lot to talk about, and so it was well after three o'clock in the afternoon when we finally climbed on board the Gemini and took off for Salisbury. It was less than a two-hour run.

Our course was southeasterly, and led us over the great Zambezi River not far from the Kariba Dam. The river lies in the bottom of a valley at least ten miles wide. It gives some idea of the huge flow of water there must have been in those primeval days, when its course had first been gouged out of Africa. Now, from our height, it looked like no more than a mere trickle at the bottom of a bath. Ahead lay the southern rim of the valley, about 4,000 feet high. Here we crossed the frontier into Southern Rhodesia. Only an hour to Salisbury.

Then ahead, right in our path, we quite suddenly became aware of a huge thunderhead massing before us. It seemed to grow as we watched it, spreading out north and south until it must have been 100 miles across. The cumulus peaks bubbled up to about 20,000 feet. They were sunlit and inviting, but the heavy flat base, dark and ominous, was not. Suddenly there was a frightening flash. A big ribbon of forked lightning cut through the cloud, to discharge with a roar somewhere on the ground beneath.

We had been warned not to fly in the afternoon. It was then that these storms developed. But seeing a cloudless sky over Lusaka, we had foolishly pressed on. The wisest thing, of course, would have been to have turned back, but I don't remember that this ever entered my head. Could we get around the thing? To the north and south the sky was clear. But the storm was huge. It might take hours, and we didn't know which way it was moving. I decided to come down under the cloud and push on through the rain.

There is something awe-inspiring about a big tropical thunderstorm. The face of the thing confronts you like a wall, brooding, daring you to tangle with it. It is, in fact, a gigantic hot-air engine, boiling with inner vortices that swirl upwards with such force that they can easily break the wings off an aircraft. Even in northern latitudes these storms are not to be trifled with. Sailplanes, striving for altitude records, sometimes enter them deliberately, cir- cling in their up-currents, blind-flying, to emerge at their summit, which, in one case at least, topped 30,000 feet. From one such sailplane, its wings torn off, the pilot jumped, his parachute opened, he thought he was falling, but the currents were actually carrying him up and it was five hours before, with frostbitten hands and feet, he finally came down.

That gives some idea of the inner forces that rumble and roar within these monsters, and you feel very small, a mere gnat, confronting their power. This is David and Goliath with a vengeance.

So the moments as we approached the black base of the thunderhead were tense. It really did feel like a dragon that was out to get us. Then we were into it. Swallowed up in the maw of the cloud. Huge raindrops exploded against the perspex like bullets. A moment later, sudden as a shout, the cloud seemed to burst open, orange, like a furnace door. We were being sucked into the weird molten glare, deep in the heart of the thing. We were losing height rapidly, but the earth beneath was hidden in the blinding downpour, which was rattling like a hundred demons against the windscreen, driving us into the ground. It was impossible to see where cloud ended and rain began. Another flash, and the furnace opened. A thunderous roar as from some furious monster. Another, and another and another. It was terrifying. This was no place to be. We must get down somehow, somewhere. Now we were under 1,000 feet. I flung the machine this way and that, desperately looking for somewhere to land.

"There's a white circle!"

It was Olga whose sharp eyes had seen it as we banked. It was wonderful, a piece of life-saving luck. For that white circle could only mean one thing. It marked a landing strip. A landing strip probably used as an emergency airfield during the war, when hundreds of young pilots had been sent down to this part of the world to complete their training in the beautiful sunny climate. They ought to have seen it that day.

"Marvelous," I shouted, and we plunged for it. I knew the place would be deserted now, but at least it must be flat and open. We shot across it at 100 feet, and the cattle grazing stampeded and left it clear. Then we circled, peering through the storm, dropped the undercart, steadied up, jammed on full flap and we were down.

We let her roll to rest, switched off and just sat there, pretty glad to be all in one piece, safe on the dear old earth. The rain continued to thunder on the cabin top, but it was waterproof. We didn't give a damn. We'd made it. We were safe. Olga had saved us in the worst forced landing I've ever had to make. I hugged her.

"Nice work, darling, you saved our bacon."

"The rain's thinning. Can't we take off again?"

"In this mud? Not on your life. We're stuck here until morning. When the sun dries it off, we'll have a go."

"We've got two bars of chocolate and two bananas."

"Fine. We'll sleep right where we are."

We looked out over the strip. As the rain thinned and the storm moved on, we could make out it was pasture, pretty firm, with some big trees at the far end. In all Rhodesia we couldn't have stumbled on a better place. It was a fantastic bit of luck. The little cabin was cosy, there was plenty of leg room, the seats were comfortable, it would be no hardship to spend the night here. The country around us appeared to be entirely deserted. In this part of the world there mightn't be anybody for miles. It didn't matter. The only thing on my mind was that I ought to get on the phone to Salisbury somehow and let them know we were down, otherwise, as our departure had been signaled out of Lusaka, they might be looking for us. But no use worrying about that. There probably wasn't a phone from here to Salisbury anyway.

Then we saw the truck.

It was old and battered and, as far as we could see, was being pushed by three native boys. With the engine revving and banging, whoever was driving it was obviously getting stuck every five yards. Then, when the boys had managed to move it on to get a better grip, it shot away and they ran after it, jumped onto the tailboard and hung on while it slithered and slipped over the fields toward us. Nobody who has not sloshed about in it can have much idea of what African mud can be after a heavy rain. It sticks to everything, caking wheels and mudguards and people indiscriminately. It's almost impossible to get through it without chains, and this truck had none. But eventually, after sliding wildly from side to side, sending up fountains of red mud from beneath it, the wretched thing drew up in front of the Gemini. The door squeaked open, and a tiny, wiry little woman of about fifty popped out.

She evidently didn't quite know what to make of the situation, and couldn't see us properly inside the cockpit. So, sliding open the window, I called out, "Good afternoon. Where are we?"

"Rondeklip. My man se plaats. Bly om jou kennis te-maak. Van der Merve is the name."

Her man may have owned Rondeklip, but you wouldn't have thought it to look at her. She was dressed in a tattered old mac, torn up one side and hanging open, a pair of gumboots several sizes too large for her, and a sort of tartan beret that was clamped over her head like a hair net. Her plain bony face was alive with curiosity.

"How is it with your wife?" She peered through at Olga.

I assured her my wife was quite all right and I was all right. We had come down because of the storm.

"Ya. We need the rain." She nodded, quite oblivious of what it meant to us.

"You English?" she asked. It was almost an accusation.

I told her that we were, on our way from London to Johannesburg, but evidently this was quite beyond her. "My magtig," she said. "You're not hurt. We heard your engine. My kaffirs saw you land. 'My God!' I said to Pa. 'Hulle's dood! They're dead!' 'If they're alive,' he said, 'bring them home.' "

I told her how grateful we were for her coming out to see if she could help, but we were quite all right. If we could just stay here until tomorrow morning . . .

"Stay here till tomorrow morning? Our home is there!" and she swung her arm toward the trees. "Daa—arsol!" The last word was so drawn out and decisive it was evident we were being offered hospitality that could not be ig-nored. "You come along. My man will be pleased to meet you." So we thanked her, and with somewhat mixed feelings threw a few things into our overnight bag, climbed out of the cockpit onto the wing, locked the windows and stepped down gingerly into the mud. Our rescuer thrust out a hand. "Bly om jou kennis temaak."

Olga replied to the formal greeting with, "How sweet of you to come and rescue us," and we started for the truck.

It wasn't that we were well dressed, but flying isn't a dirty way of travel and at least we were clean. The woman looked at Olga's cotton frock and my creased flannels without approval. It was clear to her that we were aliens—English aliens.

We were to learn later that the Afrikaners—and by her account we knew Frau Van der Merve to be one—had never quite forgiven the English for the Boer War. The British settler still has strong ties with the old country which he calls "home." But the Dutch settler had severed his ties with Holland long ago. His language is a dialect that someone from the Netherlands can hardly understand. For the Afrikaner, Africa is home.

"I can see you're not farmers," was all she said, as we picked our way over to the truck and climbed into the cab. The seats were filthy, the springs bursting through the rexine, the door had a loop of wire to hold it shut, the floor was caked with mud, the whole thing was on its last legs.

She called out, "Piet! Johannes! Kry die baas se sak!" The boy called Piet grabbed our bag. His smiling, delighted face disappeared with it into the back of the truck. There he and Johannes would hang on as best they could—when they were not out in the mud, shoving. Frau Van der

Merve got in, banging the door. One of the boys thumped on the roof. The self-starter ground, the engine roared, the wheels spun—and we remained precisely where we were.

"Piet! Johannes! Sho—vaaa . . . !"

The wheels spun, the boys shoved, the truck slithered forward, they ran after it laughing and shouting. We were off.

Lotte Van der Merve took us to a telephone. I can't remember where it was. All I retain is a wooden shed, a box on the wall with a handle to turn, an old brass receiver such as I hadn't seen since childhood. The lightning had somehow managed to find its way into the line, giving me shocks in the ear. I couldn't get through to Salisbury, but an operator somewhere along the line promised to pass on the message. Then we skidded and slithered on along the mud to the farm.

They say that one half of the world doesn't know how the other half lives, and I'm sure we must have seemed as strange to them as they did to us. Flying half across the world, completely detached from all life below us, we had suddenly been pitchforked into a microcosm of that life. It certainly gave us a jolt.

These people were Boers, that is to say third, fourth, fifth generation Dutch settlers who had first come out to the Cape and then gradually spread out over South Africa. Some families, lured by cheaper land, had even gone further north, over the border, to settle in Rhodesia. This family was an example. They were evidently very poor. The midden came right up to the doors of the tumbledown farm. In it, three or four lads, sons of the family, were sloshing about barefoot, bringing in the cattle. The animals were sad and thin, and a general air of slovenly squalor pervaded the place. The midden mud had a very ripe odor, and the boys brought it all into the house on their bare feet; it made the smell of their tightly-closed living room almost unbearable.

But of course they never noticed this. They did everything they could to look after us. We must have seemed like visitors from another planet, and when we tried to tell them something about our trip they sat with open mouths. It was clear they had no idea at all of the outside world. Italy, Greece, the Mediterranean, those were just words; they meant nothing to them whatever. The Nile—where was the Nile? "Somewhere up there." One of the lads waved a hand. Nothing outside the farm meant anything to them. I doubt if any of them had ever been educated at all.

The height of their hospitality was to offer us, after the evening meal, some cream. "Would we like some cream?" They produced a jug of it, carefully, as if it were gold. We didn't quite know what to say, as there was obviously nothing to take it with. Olga got the idea before I did. She took a spoon, dipped it into the cream, sipped it and pronounced it delicious. I did the same. It was, I suppose, the equivalent of offering us a liqueur.

The room they gave us was bare and whitewashed. Two beds, and that was all. No chairs, tables or curtains. The mattresses were of straw, the linen as coarse as canvas. We were wakened at dawn with a large tin of sweet tea, with instructions to throw out the dregs and use it to clean our teeth in. We should find water in the tap outside.

It was a glorious morning. The sun was hot and the earth was quickly drying off. We set out in the truck back to the landing field. It looked much smaller than I had thought, and although the ground was fairly firm, I didn't think we should risk a takeoff with a full load. It was then that a neighbor turned up with a bigger and better truck. He was just off to Salisbury with a load of hides, and it gave me an idea. Would he have room for our luggage, and take my wife along with him? Some 300 pounds lighter, I was sure I should have no difficulty with takeoff.

So it was agreed. We off-loaded the suitcase and all our gear, and Olga set off to Salisbury, a distance of about eighty miles. By now the day was very hot and the kind neighbor had omitted to say that his hides were fresh and bloody. They began to reek in the sun. The stench was unbearable. Olga told me afterwards how she made some excuse to get the man to stop at a chemist in the first town, to buy some tissues and eau de cologne. Dousing the tissues with it, she spent the entire journey with a pad over her nose. It made her conversation monosyllabic, and disappointed the poor man, who evidently had hoped to have a diverting exchange with his beautiful passenger.

I took off without difficulty an hour later. In forty minutes I had landed at Salisbury, taken a taxi to the Hotel Stanley, booked a room, and was sitting in the lounge waiting for Olga when she at last arrived. She was evidently pretty desperate, but at the time, knowing nothing of the stench of the hides, I couldn't quite understand why. We gave the man who had been so kind and helpful some lunch. I couldn't help noticing that he had a powerful odor, but it was only when he'd gone and we went up to our room that I fully realized the awful morning she'd had.

"I must get the smell out of my hair," she said. "I must have a bath. I stink all over. It's ghastly."

When we tried to run the bath nothing came out of the taps. It was only then we heard there was a drought. All we could get was two cans of cold water. Olga nearly cried with misery and frustration. It was days before she felt clean again.

So ended our only unscheduled stop on the trip. When, some months later, we started farming ourselves and had Boer neighbors, though they lived far more roughly and simply than we did, none, I am glad to say, were quite so primitive as that kindly family we dropped in on, half way to Salisbury.

14

To Joburg

WE STAYED THREE WEEKS in Rhodesia, hiring a car and quartering the country quite thoroughly, looking for possible farms. The character of the landscape was quite different from Kenya. There was nothing exotic about it. It was fine open country, farmed for the most part by settlers who were straightforwardly British, ranching their cattle, or growing tobacco. They were very friendly and hospitable, but our impression was one of struggle. Rhodesia was clearly going to develop, but there was still a long way to go. Everything seemed to center round Salisbury, Bulawayo, and, to a lesser extent, Umtali, and between them were miles of empty country, linked by indifferent roads, often no more than two cement tracks laid in the earth to take the wheels of cars. The African natives had their reserves dotted about the country. They seemed a cheerful, happy lot. There was none of that electrical menace we felt in Kenya.

All these opinions were, of course, very superficial. We were not in the country long enough to learn either the nature of Africa's real problems, or its possibilities. We had to trust an instinctive reaction, which was that while we felt "at home" there, as an entity Rhodesia was undercapitalized. You could buy land, but a "farm"—that is, developed property—was difficult to find. Our friends back in England, who would later come out to join us, were none of them farmers. We hoped to develop crafts, but for these we needed buildings, light, power and water. The capital overheads would be heavy. Beyond all this was the question of markets. We had to be self-supporting. With such a small English population, to whom should we sell?

It was another aspect of our problem—what sort of a place were we looking for? And we still couldn't answer it. So finally we decided to push on south and have a look at the Union. We might have to retrace our steps, but since our object was reconnaissance, we ought to cover all the ground we could.

During our stay in Rhodesia we made several local flights, quartering the country to see if we could spot likely farms. On these trips I noticed one feature that seemed peculiar to the country. There were broad sweeping

plains, but out of them, here and there, rose isolated outcrops—islands—evidently made of harder rock which had
resisted the erosion of the primeval seas and floods that
had smoothed out all the rest. But what was curious about
these outcrops was that they were carefully and elabo-
rately terraced. Stone walls grew out of their hillsides,
following the contours right up to the summits. At one
time, evidently, though they were deserted now, they
must have been cultivated, necessary to life.

But why? Why, with hundreds of square miles of fertile
land all around them, had people bothered to construct
these battlements? It was a mystery and remained so until,
many years later, I happened to come across a book by the
archaeologist H. S. Bellamy, *Built Before the Flood.* The
subject was abstruse. It concerned a very curious monument, surviving from a remote age, near the shores of
Lake Titicaca, high in the Andes. This monument, a huge
monolith of granite-like stone, was a temple gateway, dis-
playing on one side what appeared to be a stone calendar,
fashioned with extraordinary skill. Twelve formalized
"faces" each radiated a halo of twenty-four hieroglyphs.
Though there were divisions and repetitions which corre-
sponded to months and days, and even indications of
moonrise and moonset, the whole thing did not make
sense, since it added up to a 290-day year.

The temple gate of the Sun god remained an unsolved
mystery for many years until a maverick Viennese cos-
mologist, Hans Hoerbiger, waded in with a strikingly original theory. Suppose, he said, the earth had pulled in

another moon before the present one. Circling nearer and nearer to the earth, its gravitational pull would act as a brake and slow up the earth's rotation. This could result in a "year" of only 290 days. Then everything would fall into place and the calendar would make sense.

He gave other indications of this cataclysmic age. Lake Titicaca is a salt-water lake. Its various levels down the ages are clearly marked with salt encrustations on the rocks. How had a salt lake been formed 15,000 feet up in the Andes? Suppose, Hoerbiger suggested, there had been a previous moon, closer to the earth; what would its effect be? It would pull the seas up into a huge girdle tide, a hump of water around the equator. 15,000 feet would then be sea level. Such a situation must have lasted for centuries. People do not carve elaborate stone calendars for something that will change in a few months. Gradually, perhaps over thousands of years, this huge satellite was drawn closer and closer to the earth, spinning faster and faster, eclipsing the sun every other day, until finally it disintegrated in a hail of meteorites and shooting stars; an event which is faithfully recorded in the Book of Revelation.* Then, the gravitational pull gone, the seas sank back in a global cataclysm to cover the earth again. Vast areas were flooded, new continents emerged. This was when Noah took to the Ark, survived the catastrophe and repeopled the earth.

*Revelation 8:5–13 and 9:1–3, 6. The exalted character of the writing may flow from the greatness of this cataclysm which befell the earth.

Now Rhodesia is about 20° south of the equator. The girdle tide would not be so deep there. Could these terraced uplands have been isolated islands, lapped by seas which covered all the plains? Then, after these seas receded, the hills would be deserted in favor of the fertile land below.

Well, it's a fascinating theory, a glimpse perhaps of those far-off days when man existed in totally different conditions, in a world "built before the flood."

Since leaving England we had crossed many frontiers without taking much notice of these arbitrary divisions of the world, but the border between Rhodesia and the Union of South Africa was one you could not miss. Suddenly the whole character of the earth was different. This was due to clearing and cultivating on a huge scale. So much work had been put into the land, it made Rhodesia look like virgin veld. There were patterns of fields under plough or pasture, enormous plantations of citrus like dark green corduroy, standing neat and groomed. There were many farms, roads and tracks converging on small clusters of buildings where towns were springing up. Perhaps it was only the sudden contrast to the bush and jungle of the north, but the impression was vivid. The Union was way ahead of anything we had seen in Africa.

Yet, if you look at the map of the whole continent, South Africa, all those 10,000s of square miles of it, seems very small in comparison with the equatorial area to the north, much of it unexplored and unmapped, all of it practically undeveloped. The black continent may well turn out to be the untapped treasure house of the world to come. As we flew into the Union that morning, the marks of energy and wealth were plain to see. Wide motor roads began to appear, all leading south; and after two hours the cloudless sky began to thicken at the horizon to a haze which could only indicate some form of urban development. This must be Pretoria, the capital of the Union. We passed it on our left. Less than an hour to Joburg.

So we were coming to the end. 6,000 miles across the world. Fourteen days of actual flying. Apart from a few anxious moments and one forced landing, it had been a perfectly uneventful trip. But there was a deep satisfaction about it all the same, the satisfaction of bringing it to a successful conclusion. So it would always stand an indelible landmark in the memory.

In China, almost thirty years before, I thought I had come to the end of my flying days, but twenty-five years later, in another war, I had gone back to it, taken to it as smoothly as a duck to water, and learnt to fly more accurately and skillfully than I had done when I was a boy. But now I was pushing fifty. It was unlikely I should sit at the controls again. There is a time for everything—and an end to it. This was goodbye.

But of course, that morning, such thoughts never entered my head. I didn't see all those years in perspective, and hold these moments, living and precious, like a final coda to a skill I had loved so much. The wonder of flight had colored my whole life. Well, it was good to go out with a flourish. Somebody, I hoped, up there in the empyrean, was lifting a trumpet to sound a retreat for me.

But if they did, I didn't hear it. Instead I watched the ugly pyramids of yellow mud looming up on the horizon, the sludge of the gold mines, and studied the map to locate the subsidiary airfield reserved for private planes. I was occupied, as we all are, even at important moments, with the trivia of life, and could not step back even for a moment to see at the end of a long, long vista the figure of a gangling boy of sixteen, standing outside a shed at Hounslow in 1915, saying to the god at his side who was really a pilot, "Could you give me a flip around, sir—just to see if I can get my legs under the joystick?"

From that it had all begun.

15

The Safe Deposit

AS AN AID to finding a spot on which our community might settle, the Gemini had hardly been used. But it had been an inspiring way to arrive in South Africa, and the trip had cost us nothing, for we sold the airplane to the Director of Civil Aviation of the Belgian Congo at £100 more than we'd paid for it; and that exactly balanced our fuel bill.

Those whose interest lies only in flying will find nothing further in these pages to hold their attention. But, as I have said earlier, the flight was only incidental to our main purpose: that of founding a small community, so situated that it might serve as a "safe deposit" for certain ideas which were important to us.

Our leader firmly believed—and had persuaded us—that a holocaust would overtake Europe within a few years, and that finding a suitable site and preparing people to come through the disaster safely, preserving these ideas, was a sacred task entrusted to us.

Although in hindsight the whole venture seems ill-judged, impractical, and pathetically amateur, it is worth pointing out that only the timing was wrong. Today a greater threat hangs over the whole world. It seems as if some dreadful cancer has taken a death grip on mankind and is spreading at accelerating speed. Its symptoms are violence, greed and corruption, all justified by monstrous hypocrisy and blind stupidity. "Whom the gods wish to destroy, they first make mad." A terrible price may have to be paid for such heedless self-indulgence. Gurdjieff has said that our solar system is now passing through a periodic climax of tremendous tension. This shows itself in wide variability in solar activity, in sunspots, atmospheric disturbances, volcanic eruptions, earthquakes, droughts, floods and climatic irregularities. In man it produces two opposite effects: on the one hand an insatiable impulse to destroy, on the other a deep, instinctive impulse toward spiritual growth. Both impulses can be clearly seen today. On which of them predominates, the future of our civilization depends. If we wake up to our madness, the development of life on earth can enter a new phase; if not, it will be difficult to escape self-destruction and the end of all we have built up. Life will be reduced to its beginnings. The choice is ours.

In the meantime there may be some who are curious to know how our unlikely adventure fared, and how it ended. We had embraced the challenge, taken the opportunity and committed ourselves to the project. Why? Trying to put myself back into those far-away days, I find I continually return to one basic idea. It came up in conversation back in London with John Bennett a year before. We were speaking of the parlous state of the world, how it was growing worse and worse, and it seemed there was nothing anyone could do about it. "You can do nothing to set the world to rights; but you can do something to set yourself to rights. If you are all right, the world will be all right."

This idea struck me with enormous force. It changed my life. I had always looked outward—if this were changed, if that were improved, if the other were prohibited, etc. etc. It was a sort of revelation to see that society was composed of thousands of individuals who collectively produce governments, movements, trends and so on. Each played a minute part in the whole, but if every individual behaved differently, the total result would be different. It all depended on me.

This fundamental reversal of attitude, where to place the blame, where to look for the remedy, inward, not outward, became from that moment the mainspring, the principle of all my thought, and indeed, the chief directing force of my life.

I suppose it must be one of the oldest ideas in the world. But when, in my schooldays, the Church told me I was a miserable sinner and that there was no health in me, it left me cold. I, the son of two generations of parsons, would have nothing to do with it. Sin to me was theft or murder, and I was not guilty of that. And as to health, it just wasn't true; I was a very healthy young man. But now I saw there could be sins of motive, sins of attitude, sins of thought; all these if I looked inward, not outward. This was the key to change. From that point of view, everything was different. Besides, there was something I could do about it. I could change. All I had to do was to find out how. And this was where Gurdjieff came in.

How to change! It was the mainspring of Gurdjieff's teaching. Without escaping from an absolutely mechanical way of life, without *waking up,* nothing was possible. The idea is not new. It is basic to all serious religions, expressed in different ways. The Gospels are full of it. But we do not see it, because we have grown into the habit of looking at sacred books literally, never pondering what is the true meaning, the inner message of the words. So the idea that we are asleep sounds preposterous, ridiculous, we do not even bother to examine it. Besides, we cannot believe that our lives are literally all dreams, fantasies, empty of meaning; that is too much for our egos, our self-importance, our pride. And that is why change, which, as a concept, seems so desirable, turns out to be a cross when you come to grips with it. And that is why it has been so constantly ignored by generations and generations of men.

But while Gurdjieff faced us with "the terror of the situation," he also brought hope. And not only hope, but practical help, the means by which, if we worked at it, we would be enabled to wake up. He himself was a living example of what powers a man could attain to when he was fully awake, and saw the world and people around him, and saw himself most of all, *as he was,* real, not the dream we all have that we are what we think we are.

From this lifetime of search, struggle and effort, from the hidden corners of the world, he had been shown truths that had been lost or forgotten, and these he now brought back to share with all those who would work to understand them. Thus, he disclosed a marvelous system of world laws and world maintenance, that is, the way the Universe itself was put together, re-created and maintained itself. At the same time, he unfolded a detailed dissection of man and the way he is made and can grow. "You have no idea," he said, "of the possibilities of man, and the powers he is capable of attaining."

But the price of this treasure, this "kingdom of heaven," is a persistent untiring struggle with yourself: not to forget the aim; not to sleep; to live and die honorably, not "perish like a dog."

So we had blithely entered on the trail of the saints, and though we still had a long way to go, it was the certain hope that we could earn this liberation that made all the struggle more than worthwhile. That was the reason we had come to Africa, into conditions and a way of life strange to us, in the certainty that it was essential to the world to come that all these hopes should be preserved and survive.

•

But our place of retreat had still to be found. Rita had rejoined us, so now we bought a car to make a tour of the Union, drove the 1,000 miles down to the Cape, followed the coast around to Durban, and came back via Pieter-maritzburg to our starting point. We saw a lot of glorious country, a lot of properties, but nothing that seemed suit-able to our purpose. Then suddenly, on a weekend trip to the eastern Transvaal, we fell on exactly what we wanted.

Just beyond Machadadorp the 5,000-foot plateau of the High Veld breaks down in a hundred valleys and gorges to the Low Veld, the Kruger National Game Reserve, Por-tuguese East Africa, and the Indian Ocean. It is a spectacu-lar stretch of country, sparsely inhabited by a few Boer farmers. After dark not a light shows, and the timeless landscape of mountain and valley seems to stand as it has been for 10,000 years; magnificent, lonely, awe-inspiring.

Keith, Rita's husband, now joined us. He already had business interests in South Africa, and decided to buy three farms. He kept one on the High Veld to develop himself, sold the second, and presented the third to us. If to preserve Gurdjieff's ideas in a remote retreat was our aim, this farm could hardly have been bettered. To reach it, you took the track which rose over the lonely 6,000-foot ridge of the Witrand, so wind-swept and rocky that hardly a tree grew, and then dropped suddenly in a series of scary loops around sheer precipices, down through the fords of various streams into a glorious valley hemmed in by mountains. Out of a side gorge a 100-foot waterfall fell to a rock pool, forming the source of the Crocodile River. The farm chosen for our community lay in this valley bottom. In the rainy season the swollen streams made the fords almost impassable. Rocks and debris cascaded down on the higher gradients of the track. To make the thirty-mile trip to the Dorp was a slow and hazardous undertaking in a three-ton truck. But over this track every single thing required for the future community would have to be carried in. The farm was called Donkerhoek—the Dark Place. It was aptly named.

Quite undaunted by the difficulties, we set to work. My son and his beautiful young wife joined us, fresh from their honeymoon at the Rupi. Together we began to plan and build small houses for the others who would follow. My son was an excellent carpenter and a natural builder and organizer. I drew out the simple plans, and soon the little thatched places began to go up. Because a weaver formed part of our community at home, it was decided that weaving should be the first of the activities that would make our group self-supporting. South Africa abounded in sheep, nobody was weaving fine cloth, and it would certainly command a good price. Three big handlooms were ordered and shipped. But our weaver had neglected to in-

quire into the quality of South African wool. Now it tran-
spired that the sheep there were all merinos: their wool
was much too fine to be woven into the coarse tweed
necessary to tailor suits, coats and skirts and so on. So our
wool would have to be imported, spun and dyed, from
Bradford! What would happen to our supplies when the
promised cataclysm burst over Europe's head? We
shrugged that off and built a fine big mill. Then the
weaver, his wife and three children arrived and were installed. My daughter and an elderly spinster who was "interested in the ideas" joined us. Now the community was
complete.

All this of course had cost a great deal of money. The
land itself had been a present, but the buildings, the looms,
the cost of travel and the living expenses fell largely on the
people at home, on whom constant demands were made
to keep us, the pioneers, afloat. We wrote home frequently, and the picture we gave of the conditions and the
efforts being made, although perhaps to be admired, was
sufficiently intimidating to make many privately resolve
that nothing on earth would induce them to get involved
in such a setup.

We felt very much isolated and alone, and a long period
of frustrating delays followed. Through all that year we
tried, of course, to keep our work alive. We met to read
and practice the exercises taught us. But having no one
with authority who attracted our unquestioned respect,
discussion easily developed into argument. Each of us understood better than the other. We could help neither

each other nor ourselves. It was, of course, inevitable that it should be like this. But though we felt baffled and lost, we looked forward to the arrival of more people. If only we could get our activities started, everything, we thought, would be all right. Then at last the looms were delivered and erected. After further delay the wool arrived, we excitedly set up the looms, and weaving started. Then, only a week later, a freak windstorm, funneling down the deep narrow valley, lifted the roof clean off the mill to fall with a crash, smashing the looms beneath . . . !

It was a disaster. But we could not look back. Somehow or other we got the wreckage sorted out, propped up the rafters to save the total loss of the looms, stacked the thatch, cleaned the bricks, and rebuilt the whole mill on a smaller scale. In the emergency (as usual) everybody behaved splendidly. My son skillfully repaired the looms, and within a few weeks the mill was functioning again . . .

Looking back afterwards on this tough primitive life, what seems striking was the absolute trust with which we accepted our situation. One aspect of this was that nobody, as far as I can remember, ever considered Gurdjieff himself as a man, or wondered what had happened to him. He was always a mythical figure, legendary, unreal. We knew that Ouspensky had studied with him in Russia during the First World War; John Bennett himself had studied under Ouspensky, and was now passing on all he could remember to us. But what had happened to Gurdjieff? It never occurred to us to inquire why he had disappeared, where he had disappeared to, or the place and manner of his death. We did not really think of him as a living person, but only as a Master who had bequeathed to the world an extraordinary set of ideas. Here all our interest was concentrated. From one or two anecdotes that reached us about him, the dynamic force of the man sounded frightening. We were relieved in a way that we should not have to face that; his ideas were quite explosive enough for us.

The apparently simple demand to wake up, to "remember yourself always, everywhere," turned out to be well nigh impossible. Even using all the various aids given to help us, we began to see that we were faced with a summons which, though we never doubted its validity, was too heavy to bear without continual help from those who had "passed the barrier" and could support and encourage us. Naïvely lost in the African bush, we had imagined the difficult to be easy. Now, as we learned it wasn't, things went from bad to worse: relationships deteriorated; we were hardly on speaking terms; the great hope had almost reached despair.

Then, into this desperate situation came disastrous news —disastrous only from our point of view—GURDJIEFF WAS NOT DEAD! He was alive, very much alive, and was calling all who had ever known him, or followed his ideas, back to him in Paris.

16

The Death of Gurdjieff

THIS NEWS BURST ON US like an explosion. At first we were quite stunned: we could not believe it. This was very soon followed by consternation. At one blow it shattered the whole reason for our coming to Africa! Why struggle to preserve a poor copy of a masterpiece when the original is alive, and not only alive, but has set down in his own hand (as we very soon heard) all he wanted to teach, with a power and completeness that made the crumbs on which we were feeding a starvation diet?

Of all this we were made aware in the streams of letters which reached us in our far-away wilderness. The overall impression was one of joy. He was there! Alive! Among them! In his presence everything seemed to be made new. They described vividly the tiny flat near the Arc de Triomphe where all this was happening: the shuttered windows, the close atmosphere in the overcrowded room where long readings from his work took place. But most of all they described the meals.

> The arrangement of the table was formal. Gurdjieff sat at the far end, and beside him on his left was the Director of the feast. The Director had to see that everything went smoothly, that no one was without food or drink, etc.; he had to look after Gurdjieff, changing his plates and carrying out his instructions about various details, giving the toasts in a clear voice when the time came. The ritual of the toasts was drawn from what Gurdjieff called the "Science of Idiotism." He explained that in a Sufi community, a method of teaching had been handed down from antiquity which consisted in tracing the path of man's evolution from a state of nature to the realization of his spiritual potential. There are twenty-one gradations of reason from that of the ordinary man to that of our Endlessness, that is, God. No one can reach the Absolute Reason of God, and only the Sons of God like Jesus Christ can have the two gradations of reason that are the nineteenth and twentieth. Therefore the aim of every being who aspires to perfection must be to reach the eighteenth gradation . . . The word "idiot" has two meanings: the true meaning given to it by the ancient sages was *to be oneself.* A man who is himself looks and behaves like a madman to those who live in the world of illusions, so when they call a man an idiot they mean he does not share their illusions. Everyone who decides to work on himself is an idiot in both meanings. The wise know he is seeking

reality. The foolish think he has taken leave of his senses ... Gurdjieff had a fixed ritual in proposing the toasts of the idiots. He made constant use of it in his Teaching.*

The little dining room, which in the ordinary way would have been large enough to seat six people, was crammed with twenty, thirty, forty people. Those who could sit, sat, the rest stood; and the meals came in, passed from hand to hand from the diminutive kitchen. How the cooks prepared those meals was a sort of miracle in itself, for the fare was always rich and strange; too rich for the English who, in 1947–9, were still rationed to a meager diet. While he plied his guests with food, calvados and vodka, and strange delicacies of all kinds, he himself ate practically nothing. In that room, said the letters, you could not hide. It was a place of truth. No lies could exist before him. People had the feeling that he placed them, as it were, on the palm of his hand and weighed them with a look that saw them as they were. There was at the same time a homely, family atmosphere. What he said seemed phrased in such a way that there was something to be learned from it by each, whatever his level of understanding. Far from being pompous, aloof or austere, the room, we were told, vibrated with laughter; and with it a sense of life being lived at

*J. G. Bennett, *Gurdjieff, Making a New World*, Turnstone Press, 1973.

quite another level. It was a time, as one of his pupils said later, when she understood the meaning of the biblical phrase, "The Word became flesh and dwelt among us."

> All the meals are a leisurely affair, for this is G.'s time for relaxation. After the meal is finished we all go into the "salon" and settle ourselves on the chairs, on the divan, the stools or the floor. G. sits in his chair and Lise brings him his little portable organ which he rests on his knee, playing with one hand while he works the bellows with the other.
>
> He then makes the strangest music—the most wonderful music. He says it is "objective"—that is, the vibrations he produces have a definite effect on people, both organically and psychologically. It affects people in different ways. Tough businessmen and scientists sit with the tears streaming down their faces. Others are merely bored or puzzled, others again are moved but do not know exactly how.
>
> Dr Bell asked him once about this music, saying she found she did not listen to it with her ears. He said "Ears are no good for this music. The whole presence must be opened to it; it is a matter of vibrations," then he added, "But tears must come first." He also said that he had to put the whole of himself into making these vibrations. He is always very exhausted after playing. Often he does not play; we only have records of his music. It is difficult to believe they have all been made by the fingers of one hand.*

Countless anecdotes enlivened his letters: his strange, ungrammatical, pidgin English which nevertheless expressed exactly what he wished to convey; the rapier-like suddenness with which he would answer the unspoken

*Private letter to the author.

thought of someone at the other end of the room; the compassion which flowed from him in such a way that, however stern or ruthless he seemed, those who suffered from his blows knew them to be inflicted impartially, to help them to see, and looked on him with a mixture of awe and worship. For himself he took nothing, but he gave to all with a magnanimity they would never forget. When we sent him from Africa a tray of avocado pears (hearing that he liked them), back by air came three pound pots of Russian caviar.

From all this we were cut off. Our pioneering, apparently so important up till now, had become quite irrelevant before what was happening in Paris. We were out on a limb, and had missed an opportunity which, we felt, might have changed all our possibilities. More practically, our situation, our future, lost all interest to those at home. Our valley community depended upon them for money; we were far from self-supporting. Now all the money was required to offer hospitality to the hundreds of people who flocked to Paris.

Naturally those at home did all they could, by describing the events that were taking place and conveying something of what was taught, to help us. Some visited our lonely valley and we could see the change in them reflected from their experiences. The first chapters of *All and Everything** reached us in typescript. It was so

---

All and Everything: An Objectively Impartial Criticism of the Life of Man, or Beelzebub's Tales to his Grandson, by G. I. Gurdjieff, Routledge, Kegan Paul, 1950.

strange, like nothing we had ever read before, and quite baffling to our understanding. It was many years before we began to learn to give it its true place. "In its complexities and obscurities like an alchemical text, in its human robustness like a Rabelaisian chronicle, in its breadth like a monumental work of historical analysis, in its passion like a sermon and its compassion like something almost sacramental, *Beelzebub's Tales* surpasses all ordinary points of view."* It belongs to a new kind of thought, older than the most ancient mythologies, newer than the last word in scientific research. It speaks from another level to another kind of man, ready to stand face to face with a new vision of reality.

At that time the bewildering complexities of the teaching obscured for me the simplicity that lay at the heart of it.

For centuries the impulses of faith, hope and love have inspired all serious religions. But today these traditional ways have lost their original power to move us. They have become threadbare through common use. There is little faith, hope or love in the world today.

But there is a fourth way, the way of conscience. Conscience has been called the representative of the Creator in us and lies deep, forgotten, buried at the core of everyman's heart.

---

*A. G. E. Blake, "Preface to *Beelzebub's Tales* by John Bennett."

All the demands made on those who study Gurdjieff's work are finally directed toward this basic aim—to uncover and bring back conscience into daily living.

But not that conscience which is mere morality, subject to passing customs and laws of the day; rather the unchanging sacred impulse which, though it has been driven back within, still burns like a fire at the center of every life.

Today we have become accustomed to the almost total lack of any standards of honor, justice and compassion in the world. Yet, at the same time, twinges of remorse are beginning to disturb us, goading us toward the realization that conscience and conscience alone can inspire that revaluation of all ideals necessary to sustain us in our search for a new reality.

But in those far-off days, such a distillation was beyond us. We could not see the wood for the trees. At that time all I remember is that it aroused in me a compulsive desire to get back to Paris, to the source of that help of which we had so great a need. But, as that was impossible, we just struggled on.

Then, one morning, I was told there was a telegram for me in the Dorp. Telegrams were unusual, so my son and I drove in to get it.

"Gurdjieff died 11 o'clock, 29 October."

I stood there quite stunned. It was impossible. It couldn't have happened. I felt deprived of everything. Nothing had purpose any more. The loss was as personal as if I had lost my own father. We all felt it. That night, and for many nights afterwards, the valley fulfilled its name—the dark place.

It seemed weeks before we had any detailed news. Then letters began to arrive from which we could piece together some sort of a picture of those extraordinary last days in Paris.

Nothing perhaps better illustrates these days, and the level of his own life, than the demoniac way Gurdjieff created an ambience of uncertainty and even chaos about him. Nobody was allowed to be "comfortable." He seemed deliberately to contrive situations in which people could not remain "asleep." Continual surprises, changes of plan, contrary directions, disappointments, jealousies—he played on every facet of the human personality and threw it off balance, so that people should "wake up" and see how they reacted, how they were.

Yet when it was over, it was possible to discern behind the confusion an ordered plan that was moving steadily forward. Large sums of money had been collected to publish *Beelzebub.* Funds had been provided for his son and to endow close relatives—he took nothing, of course, for himself. The last series of his "Movements," his sacred dances, had been given. All those fortunate ones who reached Paris had been shown by his own example a new vision of life. All the aims he had set himself had been completed; his work was done.

The end, when it came, was swift and sudden. A devoted American doctor flew in from New York and rushed him to the American Hospital in Neuilly. He appeared

interested in all the gadgets and the new drugs that were
to save him. But then he seemed to withdraw from his
body. His strength ebbed. In three days he was dead.

> When we saw him in the chapel he looked most
> beautiful. When I first went in I (unexpectedly to my-
> self) quite broke down and had to go out for a minute.
> I was simply overwhelmed by the immensity of the
> event. But as I sat by him I grew stronger, and above
> all more cheerful. In the end I felt myself possessed by
> a kind of conscious well-being that was almost gay. It
> came from the immense power of his being. He lay
> there as if he had chosen consciously to put his body
> just there, and just like that.*

6,000 miles away in the wilderness, all these crumbs of
detail from Paris were collected as something very precious. We all felt bereft and deeply moved, and for a time,
struggled to achieve some feeling of unity. But feelings,
however intense, do not last. Suddenly we saw we were
quite incapable of maintaining anything useful by ourselves. The looms were sold, the whole venture disintegrated. Keith and Rita struggled to control the situation
with their usual even-tempered generosity. They took on
my son to manage their farm, my daughter returned to
England, Donkerhoek was sold. We, when we saw that the
farm we had bought nearby could never pay, sold it also
at a heavy loss. A year before, we had been forced to sell
my beloved Rupi to pay our debts. Of the £10,000 we had
put in personally, we returned to the U.K. with about

---

*Private letter to the author.

£1,000; and with this, at fifty-three, and no idea how I should earn a living, I had to start again.

I do not remember that I complained much of the situation. With what now seems to have been cheerful resilience I cast around for something to do. The thing that really counted for me above all else was that, quite undismayed by the fact that we were ruined and our life situation was desperate, I was back as near as I could get to the source of those ideas which, ever since I first heard them, had become the most important thing in my life.

So ended our great African adventure.

ABOUT THE AUTHOR

CECIL LEWIS was born in 1898 and educated at Dulwich College and Oundle. At the age of sixteen and a half he joined the Royal Flying Corps, and at eighteen he flew over the Somme battlefields. He survived three operational tours, and action in the defense of London, and was awarded the Military Cross. As a test pilot, he flew almost every type of aircraft then in use with the R.F.C. These years are described in his classic account of flying in the First World War, *Sagittarius Rising* (1936).

In 1919 he became manager of Civil Aviation Vickers Ltd. and went to Peking as a flying instructor to the Chinese government. Rejoining the R.A.F. at the outbreak of the Second World War, he spent five years in the Air Ministry as a flying instructor and finished his war service in command of staging posts in Sicily and Greece. He was one of the founders of the B.B.C., and chairman of the Program Board from 1922 to 1926. He worked for the United Nations Secretariat in New York for radio and television (1953–5), with commercial television in London (1955–6), and then with the *Daily Mail* from 1956 until his retirement in 1966.

Cecil Lewis has written for both stage and screen. For the screen he made the first two classic adaptations of Bernard Shaw's plays, and his own dramatic works for television—which he also produced—include *Nativity*, *Crucifixion*, and *Patience of Job*. Among his other publications are *Broadcasting from Within* (1924), *The Trumpet*

Is Mine (1938), *Challenge to the Night* (1938), *Pathfinders* (1943), *Yesterday's Evening* (1946), *Farewell to Wings* (1964), *Turn Right for Corfu* (1972), his autobiography *Never Look Back* (1974), which was filmed for television, and *A Way To Be* (1977).

Mr. Lewis now resides in Greece.

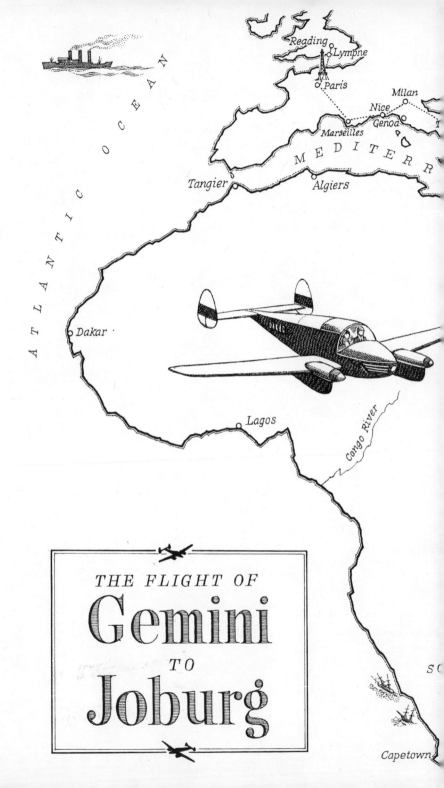

THE FLIGHT OF
Gemini
TO
Joburg